Talking About
Pop Music:
An A to Z of Hit Artists

Talking About Pop Music

Talking About Pop Music:

An A to Z of Hit Artists

By James Iles

Author: James Iles
Cover Design: jammasound
ISBN: 9789561273445
Revised Edition

Contents

Chapter	Page

Preface

When the coronavirus pandemic locked down most of the world in March 2020, my way of working, like everybody's, suddenly changed forever.

I'm the chief sub-editor of a newspaper group where half the staff got furloughed, and one of the first cuts from the company budget was our subscription to the features wire.

Thinking about how to plug the gaps in our content, I felt, with the pause button firmly pressed on gigs and festivals, readers would still need their musical fix.

It's a topic I feel passionately about and, as I will explain in the introduction, pop music has always been a key part of my life.

Brainstorming, I came up with an "A to Z" of my favourite hit artists or possibly a theme based on each letter of the alphabet gave it an immediate structure plus the possibility of up to 26 week's worth of features.

Next I wanted a catchy title that "does what it says on the tin".

"Talking About Pop Music" was an immediate thought. Yes, it's a reference to the one-hit wonder "Pop Muzik" by M, and a very literal reference to what I'd be doing. So, I went with that, supported by a sub-heading of "An A to Z of Hit Artists".

Talking About Pop Music

The "hit artists" reference bound me to writing about groups and solo stars of considerable note, not just any artist or album that fitted the letter.

And though I never set a pre-requisite record sales threshold, it certainly figured when making final choices.

I don't believe I was too partisan either. Obviously I have gone with many of my personal favourite bands and solo artists as all choices are subjective, but some weeks there were several options which posed a tough choice for me.

On other occasions I deliberately opted for a group or someone who would stretch my knowledge and I found that to be equally as enjoyable and challenging.

For example, 'D' offered up both of Depeche Mode and Duran Duran – two groups I am passionate about and have seen live many times and, while I went with the latter, the former got their own chapter later on, under 'V' for 'Violator'.

'F' for Fleetwood Mac, on the other hand, was one that taught me so much about a great band with a turbulent history who I'd always admired from afar but had always yearned to know more about.

So, that learning curve was just as rewarding as, say, pouring out all I already knew (and having to severely edit down!) about someone like 'P' for Pet Shop Boys, who would definitely be my chosen subject on *Mastermind*.

Writing the features in my own time, it soon became obvious I had so much I wanted to share about the subject of pop music than what was edited down for the papers and websites, so this book has been the perfect platform for them.

I have given some of them a "Top three" of songs (unless it is a feature that specifically looks at a set of tracks like 'N' for New Order), as well as an underrated track I wanted more people to know about, and I have kept those here where applicable to show my preferences of tracks from the artist or album.

I've also kept the online playlists I lovingly compiled on Spotify and Amazon Music here too.

I used both platforms for the compilations as some weeks I found one to be more comprehensive than the other in its coverage of an artist or album.

Those links are written with shortened urls for ease of typing into your smartphone or computer, and the playlists themselves are designed to further augment understanding of the topics.

It goes without saying that I hope readers will become listeners too, and pop on the playlists while reading the book.

I shared many of them on social media so, what started out as an idea to provide interesting content, truly did get tens of thousands of people "Talking About Pop Music" at a time when artists and fans were missing that live connection and new releases have been limited by the pandemic.

Finally, writing this book has kept me sane during lockdown. Some people went fitness crazy, read books or took up a new hobby. I wrote this book. I hope you enjoy it too!

"The year 3,000 may still come to pass,
But the music shall last,
I can hear it on a timeless wavelength,
Never dissipating but giving us strength"

Pet Shop Boys *'It's Alright'*
(Tennant/Lowe)

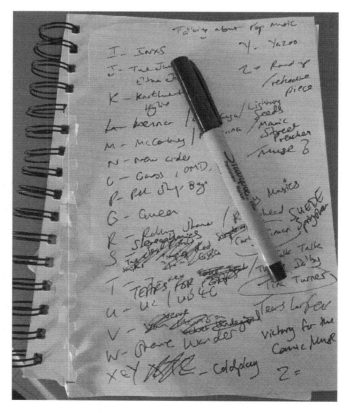

My notepad 'masterplan' for this series of features, which changed many times.

Musical Memories

FOR AS long as I can remember - probably aged around four or five - pop music has been one of my biggest passions.

Looking back, it stems, in part, from listening to the likes of The Beatles, the Everly Brothers, Buddy Holly, Abba and even those chart compilation tapes (you know, the ones earned through petrol station tokens in the 1980s) in the backseat of my parents' car.

There were more car journeys back then – setting off from our family home in Hollywood, Birmingham - in the days before people flew everywhere, or could order their shopping online and have it delivered to their door.

I count myself lucky, then, that in turn meant I was exposed to the great songs and beautiful melodies of pop and rock royalty while en route to the supermarket, visiting my grandparents or getting a few albums' worth in on the way to a seaside holiday.

Later, in my teenage years, my own tastes and those of my two brothers developed and expanded, so on went our respective headphones in what became our own private listening booths on those very same car journeys.

For me, it meant listening to those early Pet Shop Boys' albums 'Please' and 'Actually', compilations of 1980s Sunday night Top 40 chart countdowns and everything else from New Order and Prince through to Depeche Mode and The Smiths, more often than not they were taped off an original vinyl copy.

Later on, as a student in the 1990s, long train journeys to and from university were permeated with whole albums such as Blur's 'Great Escape', Oasis' 'What's The Story (Morning Glory)', 'Coming Up' by Suede and Radiohead's 'OK Computer'.

But listening had never been enough. Since I was about nine or ten, I'd wanted to understand the music I was listening to, specifically the synthesizers bands used on songs like 'Rio', 'Always on My Mind' and 'Enjoy The Silence', and I was saving up pocket money and working part-time jobs to buy all the music gear I could afford.

My parents, to my eternal gratitude, took note of this "hobby", and my devotion to it, and agreed to let me attend the Yamaha Music School in nearby Redditch in Worcestershire, UK.

Toys were swapped for sheet music on my Christmas list and my apparent "ear for music" was refined with the help of this newly-acquired theoretical musical knowledge.

I had become completely immersed in analysing not just the art of songwriting, but also the production behind my favourite pop tunes, studiously poring over the credit notes on album sleeves to learn just who it was that was behind these amazing feats of aural pleasure.

Next I set about creating my own music. This was chiefly made possible by investing all of my building society savings in a Yamaha QY-10 sequencer which I had linked up to a modest but practical full-size key Casio home keyboard using MIDI. I later also bought a QY-70, its much-improved and more expensive sibling!

I would tape my demos on to a then state-of-the-art chrome tape cassette. Years later, I was able to record in even higher quality on a mini disc recorder – a much underrated piece of kit that should have caught on better than it did.

I hesitate to admit that some of these instrumental "Jammasound" tracks still exist on Soundcloud.

There, you'll also find some demos from the university band I played organs for - "Go Bossa". And great tunes they are too, in my humble opinion!

So here is my confession – I'm a frustrated pop musician too, like millions of others.

But through this book I've got to write about it all instead, and it's been a thoroughly enjoyable process.

Nowadays, my own children are discovering their favourite artists on streaming services and social media.

But while they can make their own short music videos on apps, nothing beats the joy of cranking up your *Walkman*, or recording your own music on to an actual demo tape does it?

Talking of social media, my passion for Pet Shop Boys' music led me to set up a Facebook campaign to help them score a festive No.1 in 2009 with their 'Christmas' EP.

Alas, they did not top the pop parade (the EP format actually made it ineligible for the singles charts) however that group then morphed into something bigger – a fan-based community that now has some 6,000 members globally.

Talking About Pop Music

It's a hive of shared love for my favourite pop group, with all the latest news and gossip shared by Facebook users from the UK to the USA and from Holland to Hong Kong.

Never meet your heroes is the old cliche, but I disagree as I am really lucky to have met Pet Shop Boys - a couple of times - after patiently waiting by the stage door with scores of fellow Petheads.

The first time was in 2002 on their 'Release' tour when both Neil Tennant and Chris Lowe signed a postcard for me which was amazing, even though, sadly, this was before smartphones so, alas, no pictures exist of the meeting.

The second time was in 2007 on the 'Fundamental' tour though, strictly speaking, it was just Neil as the famously shy Chris had already swerved the fans to get straight on the tour bus!

Neil very kindly signed a rare copy of their much sought-after 1989 official annual "Pet Shop Boys, annually", remarking he didn't even have a copy himself. (A moral dilemma for me - should I have given him my copy? Apparently he does have one now!)

I'm also very lucky to have met Depeche Mode (who are very narrowly my second favourite group). This was during a recording for CD:UK which I won tickets to in 2001.

Depeche were back on the Saturday morning shows plugging 'Dream On' and 'I Feel Loved' from their 'Exciter' album and I was able to shake hands with Martin Gore, Andy Fletcher and Dave Gahan in and around the filming.

No phones or cameras were permitted though. So, again, sadly, I only have the memories. They are ones I will treasure though and I feel extremely fortunate to have met some of my musical heroes.

Last Christmas, I was fortunate to meet John Taylor and Roger Taylor from Duran Duran at a charity fund-raising ball and photographic evidence does exist - see "D is for Duran Duran".

Incidentally, I competed against the Duran duo and scores of others that night in a pop quiz, and won!

One final thought before we get on with the A to Z and "let the music play".

It's my personal musical memories that have steered the content in this book so, before you read my choices, please remember my views, like all musical choices and opinions, are entirely subjective.

I hope you enjoy the results, and if so, why not join in the discussion with me on Twitter?

My handle is *@jammasound* and the hashtag is #TalkingAboutPopMusic

Join me online "Talking About Pop Music"

on Twitter by following @jammasound

"Thank you for the music, the songs we're still singing"

'A' is for ABBA

One of my favourite childhood Christmas memories was unwrapping a copy of 'Super Trouper' by ABBA.

I can remember this moment like it was yesterday, even some 40 years later.

We already had a copy of the 1976 collection 'Abba: Greatest Hits' which had been taped for the car and was by now in a well-worn album sleeve with some songs skipping (admittedly probably because of smaller hands keenly putting the needle on the record!)

So 'Super Trouper' was something brand new to us and more songs from ABBA were very welcome.

I still love every track on this LP which captures Benny Anderson, Bjorn Ulvaeus, Agnetha Falkstog and Anni-Frid Lyngstad at the height of their pop mastery.

Revisiting it for this book, I can confirm it has all the calibre of a hits collection, even though it was actually the seventh of ABBA's eight studio albums.

Referring of course to a type of stage spotlight, the title track is a glorious slice of Europop that tells a story of the band on tour, featuring all the best hallmarks of ABBA - Benny's majestic piano,

Bjorn's thoughtful lyrics and the glorious vocals of Agnetha and Anni-Frid. Not many global hits reference Glasgow either.

Songs like the timeless and beautiful 'The Winner Takes It All' are still a go-to track for those suffering the pain of divorce as is 'Our Last Summer' while musically 'The Piper' is as hypnotically catchy as the subject matter.

'Me and I' sees a welcome embrace of synthesizers which were to be such a huge influence in the coming years.

Then there's the hit 'Lay All Your Love on Me' which later helped Erasure to number 1 in 1992 and the brilliant 'Happy New Year', a song of hope at the start of a new decade which I still listen to every New Year's Eve.

ABBA was forged in folk music roots and famously consisted of two couples (Benny and Anni-Frid / Bjorn and Agnetha).

The Swedish quartet became one of Scandinavia's biggest exports since Volvo after bursting on to the scene with a glam-rock look on their 1974 Eurovision winner 'Waterloo'.

From 1976 to 1982 they dominated the charts, particularly in Australia, the UK and USA.

The camp fun, romance and joy of their earlier hits like 'Dancing Queen', 'Ring Ring', 'Money, Money, Money', 'Mamma Mia!' and 'Fernando' gave way to more mature and considered songs later in their career.

Knowing me, knowing you - Scandinavian superstars ABBA.

No more carefree laughter

"Breaking up is never easy", but ironically for ABBA it inspired a particularly creative period of reflective and poignant songs, starting with 'Knowing Me, Knowing You', around the time Bjorn and Agnetha started to have doubts about their marriage.

"In these old familiar rooms, children will play, now there's only emptiness, nothing to say," penned Ulvaeus with a real sense of heartbreak in the 1977 hit.

Similar true-to-life songs follow, but to their credit ABBA continued to record and perform together despite marital issues.

The sweeping symphonic electronic sounds of pop novella 'The Day Before You Came', not even a top 20 hit in the UK, and synth-drenched 'Under Attack' and 'When All Is Said And Done' marked a departure from the disco and glam-rock of their 1970s heyday and a sign of the new direction Benny and Bjorn were heading with their songwriting that would also see them partner Tim Rice to create the musical 'Chess' in 1983.

ABBA are arguably valued more in hindsight - just consider the amount of greatest hits compilations, musicals, films, tribute acts and TV specials that still pervade our lives today - some 38 years since they ceased recording - having wrongly been seen as a bit unfashionable at the time. Well, the outfits didn't help.

Reunited in 2016, new music – at least five tracks, but hopefully a whole album - and a "virtual" tour have been promised soon. Fingers and bell bottoms crossed.

My top three Abba tracks
1. The Winner Takes It All
2. Waterloo
3. Voulez Vous
Underrated track = The Day Before You Came

• Check out my 'A is for ABBA' playlist on Spotify at https://spoti.fi/2RKcyNu

Author's notes: *"ABBA were the obvious choice for 'A', though ABC and A-ha were definitely strong contenders, and I really love A-ha!*

"However, ABBA's success and legacy speak for themselves and place them in a league of their own, making them the worthy choice for my first feature in the series."

"The stars look very different today,

without Bowie"

'B' is for Bowie

"IF YOU'RE sad today, just remember the earth is over 4billion years old and yet you somehow managed to be alive at the same time as David Bowie."

This quote, rightly or wrongly attributed at the time to the comedy actor Simon Pegg, felt so perfect for how the world was feeling after Bowie's untimely death in January 2016.

The enigmatic genius' final album 'Blackstar' had been released just two days earlier and while its content (including the titular song and tracks like 'Lazarus') gave a sense of foreboding that Bowie may not have long left on this planet, it did nothing to ease the shock and pain of his passing.

David Bowie influenced so many hit artists across five decades of recording music and was so often at the forefront of fashion it is hard to think of many who could say they hadn't been inspired, even indirectly, by his broad spectrum of work.

He was the master of reinvention, the chameleon of pop, and such was his timespan that it's likely a different Bowie era rings true for each of us. For me it was the 1980s that first piqued my interest in the 'Starman'.

*

I first recall David Bowie as a Pierrot-esque clown figure in a court procession of New Romantics parading up a beach for the video of 1980 smash hit 'Ashes to Ashes'.

Here, Bowie "remembers the guy that's been in such an early song" when he revisits the character of Major Tom from his first chart hit 'Space Oddity' (1969), which later went to number one as a re-release in 1975.

The video was the most expensive ever made at the time and perfectly encapsulated the arts and music scene of the period, featuring club scene characters like Steve Strange who were key to the burgeoning New Romantics move that was erupting.

Bowie was the hero of this pop culture movement – 80s stars Duran, Duran, Spandau Ballet, Depeche Mode, and so many others would all cite him as their big influence - yet, in one hit song and video, he both endorsed and reaffirmed their fashion and style as the current coolest thing on the planet.

He was a leader and a follower of cutting edge trends. 'Ashes to Ashes' was (only) his second UK No.1, and though he is known for his 1970s 'Golden Years' with hits like 'Starman', 'Life on Mars', 'Rebel Rebel', 'The Jean Genie' and 'Heroes', it's worth remembering Bowie scored three more of his five UK No.1s in the 1980s.

Chart-toppers 'Let's Dance' (1983) – brilliantly produced by Nile Rodgers – and duets with Queen on 'Under Pressure' (1981) and Mick Jagger on 'Dancin' in the Streets' (1985) were to follow. Does commercial success eclipse credibility though? You decide.

It wasn't just the number ones that defined the 80s for Bowie, he was one of the star turns at Live Aid in 1985, and his prolific career saw him release (often underrated) songs for movies like 'Cat People (Putting Out The Fire)', 'Absolute Beginners' and 'When The Wind Blows' (remember Raymond Briggs' post-apocalyptic cartoon film?). 'China Girl', 'Fame' (with John Lennon) and 'Fashion' are firm favourites from this decade too.

Ssshhh! Kirk Whitehouse recreates a famous image of David Bowie for his Smashed Hits / Broken Vinyl art collection.

Moving into the 1990s and the *Thin White Duke* was once again on the front foot, embracing the new dance music rhythms of the time which underpinned his 'comeback' hit 'Jump They Say' (from 'Black Tie White Noise') when he once again hired Nile Rodgers as producer, and Bowie himself played saxophone on top of the funky single which got to No. 9 in the UK in 1993, his only top ten between 1986's 'Absolute Beginners' and 2013's 'Where Are We Now?'

1993 also saw Bowie provide the nostalgic soundtrack to Hanef Kureshi's brilliant 'Buddha of Suburbia' TV series, the title track being a personal favourite of mine.

He gave an industrial/grungy sound to the Brian Eno-produced 'Heart's Filthy Lesson' of 1995 from the 'Outside' album which also gave us another great single when 'Hallo Spaceboy' was remixed and released as a co-performance with Pet Shop Boys, another group who acknowledge working with Bowie as a career high-point, such was his influence on them.

Giving it more than a lashing of the PSB's signature synth-dance sound, Neil Tennant also added a verse to the original Eno/Bowie song using one of Bowie's methods of writing by taking sentences (in this case from 'Space Oddity'), cutting them up and re-arranging them to make new lyrics. Thankfully Bowie approved and they performed it together at the legendary 1996 Brit Awards show.

Illness – Bowie suffered from a blocked artery on tour in 2004 prompting emergency heart surgery – saw a slowing down of his career in the 2000s though he did reunite his live band to record his penultimate band 'The Next Day' in 2013.

The release of his 27th and final studio album 'Blackstar' on January 8th 2016 - Bowie's 69th birthday - preceded his death from liver cancer by two days.

It was a reflective release, critically acclaimed, and one last treat from an artist who is peerless in his influence and inspiration on contemporary music.

Like all the best pop stars, Bowie was androgynous and mysterious which only added to his mystique.

His other-worldly persona made it hard to fathom his journey to the stars and it's difficult to see another artist who will ever come near his impact on either popular music or popular culture.

My top three David Bowie tracks

1. Ashes to Ashes
2. Life on Mars?
3. Starman
Underrated track = Absolute Beginners (Official video on YouTube)

• **Check out James' 'B is for Bowie' Spotify playlist**
at https://spoti.fi/3iO1hY5

"While The Beatles are, for many, the most clear consideration for 'B', I actually felt it was hard to say anything entirely comprehensive or original about them and always thought about looking at Lennon and McCartney separately.

"Bowie's influence is certainly on a par with the Fab Four's in my opinion."

"From new wave to the Hall of Fame,

there's only one Elvis"

'C' is for Costello

"OLIVER'S Army are on their way, Oliver's Army are here to stay, and I would rather be anywhere else but here today."

Elvis Costello's dramatic lyrics about the Northern Ireland Troubles he witnessed first-hand are notably juxtaposed against the joyous pop melody and uplifting harmonies of 'Oliver's Army' - his biggest UK hit that was kept off the No.1 spot by both the Bee Gees' 'Tragedy' and Gloria Gaynor's 'I Will Survive'.

Oliver refers to Oliver Cromwell and the song also references imperialist struggles in Hong Kong, South Africa and Palestine. But with its 1950s 'doo-wop' chord progression, topped off with Steve Nieve's jubilant piano chords (deliberately styled on Abba's 'Dancing Queen'), the song's musical style could not be further from the seriousness of the subject matter.

Taken from Costello's fine third album 'Armed Forces' (1979) 'Oliver's Army' is still a radio staple today and it broke Elvis Costello through from new wave to mainstream, but there is so much more to the body of work of this musical maestro.

*

Born Declan McManus in 1954, in Paddington, London, Costello is of Irish descent on the side of his Birkenhead-born father Ross

McManus who was also a musician - most famous for writing and singing the 'R Whites Lemonade' TV advert song (Elvis did the backing vocals!) that anyone with a TV in the 1970s and 80s will remember (it's on YouTube if you want some nostalgia).

Young Declan was raised in London until he moved to Birkenhead with his mother Lilian (originally from Liverpool) in 1971, when he was 16.

He moved back to London in 1974 and, after recording *that* TV commercial with his dad he worked at being a songwriter himself, eventually producing a demo that got him signed to Stiff Records in 1976 at which point he invented his stage name - Elvis Costello.

Chapter One

With his trademark over-sized glasses giving him a resemblance to Buddy Holly, Costello worked with Steve Nieve on breakthrough solo hit 'Watching the Detectives' (1977).

He soon added Bruce Thomas on bass and the unrelated Pete Thomas on drums to create his permanent backing band The Attractions.

Though Costello had scored a relative success with his solo debut LP 'My Aim Is True' (1977) that featured his first hit 'Alison', it was after 'This Year's Model' (1978) - his first album with The Attractions (including '(I Don't Wanna Go To) Chelsea' and 'Pump It Up') - when things started to gain pace.

Saturday Night Live brought the band in as a replacement for the Sex Pistols (new wave literally replacing punk right there folks!) but their performance was marred by controversy after Costello stopped them while starting to play 'Less Than Zero' (the agreed song) and swapped to 'Radio Radio' instead.

The latter is critical of the commercialisation of the airwaves and they were asked by NBC not to play it.

Costello was subsequently banned from the show, until 1989.

This incident is one of many politically-charged points Costello has made in his career which have marked his cards as a controversial figure at times.

In 1989 he released 'Tramp The Dirt Down', a vitriolic attack on Margaret Thatcher where he anticipates her death so he can stamp on her grave, and which he unapologetically performed at Glastonbury in 2013 following her passing that April.

'Shipbuilding', released in 1982, was a poignant ballad about the Falklands War, contrasting the killing of young British soldiers as an unintended consequence of a revival for struggling shipyards.

"Is it worth it?" he asked. "A new winter coat and shoes for the wife, and a bicycle on the boy's birthday." "Within weeks they'll be reopening the shipyards and notifying the next of kin."

Hall of fame

While his political commentaries give him credibility as an artist, his legacy of hit songs is what he will be remembered for.

Costello has recorded 25 studio albums including those with The Attractions or The Imposters, and 11 collaborative albums over his long and successful career.

Hit songs like 'Accidents Will Happen', 'I Can't Stand Up For Falling Down', 'High Fidelity', 'Every Day I Write The Book', '(What's So Funny 'Bout) Peace and Understanding' and 'A Good Year for the Roses' - the latter being a superb tribute to his love of country music - cemented his position in the public pop music psyche and led to a host of invites to collaborate from his peers including, in the late 80s, a phone call off one of his heroes – none other than Paul McCartney.

The Merseyside duo hooked up for a song-writing session for what would become McCartney's 'Flowers in the Dirt' album, including the single 'My Brave Face' (1989).

For Costello it delivered 'Veronica' (1989), another upbeat pop song set to heart-rending lyrics which is a tribute to his grandmother Mabel (her confirmation name was Veronica) and her struggle with Alzheimer's.

Costello fulfilled more ambitions and achieved more success working with the legendary Burt Bacharach on their 'Painted in Memory' LP (1998).

Costello had long been a Bacharach fan, and had recorded several Bacharach songs, beginning with 'I Just Don't Know What to Do with Myself' in the late 70s. He also recorded a credible cover of Bacharach and David's 'I'll Never Fall in Love Again' for an Austin Powers movie.

Elvis Costello as recreated by Kirk Whitehouse for his Smashed Hits Broken Vinyl art collection.

That was nothing compared to his brilliant take on Charles Aznavour's 'She' (for the movie Notting Hill).

It's no mean feat taking on such a famous song, let alone one by someone considered a pop deity which has been recorded so many times, but Costello pulled it off with aplomb.

Costello has also collaborated with Madness, Tony Bennett, Allen Toussaint, T Bone Burnett, Lucinda Williams, Johnny Cash, Kid Rock and Brian Eno.

He is listed as one of the top 100 Greatest Artists of All Time by Rolling Stone magazine, won Grammys in 1999 and 2020, was inducted into the Rock and Roll Hall of Fame in 2003, and, in 2010, had the great honour of performing 'Penny Lane' in front of President Barack Obama at The White House when Sir Paul McCartney accepted the Library of Congress Gershwin Prize for Popular Song.

My top Elvis Costello tracks

1. Oliver's Army
2. Watching The Detectives
3. A Good Year for the Roses
Underrated track = She
• Check out James' 'C is for Costello' Spotify playlist at https://spoti.fi/2RLvdbr

"A bit of an outsider's choice, but deliberately so as I feel Costello's influence on pop music is vastly underrated and more people should check out his impressive back catalogue."

"How the Wild Boys' hunger for glory forged their place as pop music legends"

'D' is for Duran Duran

WHEN two starry-eyed kids from the same sleepy housing estate just south of Birmingham discovered the joy of playing records in their bedrooms and going to gigs up town, a mutual passion for music was ignited - and so they began plotting their path to pop stardom.

The pair in question are John Taylor (then known as Nigel) and Nick Rhodes (then Nick Bates) of Hollywood, Birmingham (not LA at this point), a quiet commuter-belt village on the edge of the north Worcestershire countryside - yet only a No.50 bus ride away from the bright lights of Broad Street.

It was in that city centre - chiefly the Rum Runner club - where, amidst a melting pot of burning talent also brimming with UB40, Dexys Midnight Runners and The Beat, the future of Duran Duran was forged, as told here by another Hollywood boy - me.

*

It was 1978. Having settled on the name Duran Duran (their misheard take on the villain 'Durand Durand' from the cult movie Barbarella starring Jane Fonda) founder members John and Nick set about recruiting for the band.

They had borrowed money off parents for a guitar (John) and - crucially to their eventual sound - one of the first Wasp synthesizers in the UK for Nick. It set his mum Sylvia back £200 but it turned out to be a sage investment.

Several line-up changes later (including the departure of original singer Stephen 'Tin Tin' Duffy), the group were moulding together nicely, now with Roger Taylor (no relation to John) as their drummer.

They advertised for a guitarist as John had moved on to bass guitar allowing he and Roger to hone the groove of their disco-funk fusion rhythm section.

Another unrelated Taylor – Andy - answered the call all the way from Newcastle in April 1980, but there was just one problem – they didn't have a lead singer.

Birmingham University Drama student Simon Le Bon was suggested to the boys by Simon's then girlfriend, a barmaid at the club.

Le Bon joined them in May and, to the relief of the others, he was armed with a book of poetry that became their lyrics.

Duran Duran quickly became the house band at the Rum Runner, working there too, to earn extra money. Nick was a DJ, John worked on the door, Andy "polished mirrors and cooked burgers" while Roger was a glass collector.

They were managed by the club's owners Paul and Michael Berrow from an office above the nightspot famous for hosting David Bowie, Roxy Music and Chic nights - all artists who heavily influenced the sound of Duran Duran.

A tour supporting Hazel O'Connor followed and, by that December, a record deal with EMI.

Duran Duran broke through with their first single 'Planet Earth' hitting No.12 in the UK in 1981, the video perfectly capturing the New Romantic scene.

Being fans of the club culture and extended mixes, 'Girls on Film' (Night Mix) (1981) was tailored for the seedier side of nightlife.

Godley & Creme directed a controversial erotic video for the single (it featured topless women pillow fighting in a wrestling ring) which, while being banned on most TV stations, was played on loop in the new clubland video screens. This 'exposure' helped it become their second top ten hit, peaking at No.5 in the UK.

The Fab Five

By the time of their second album 'Rio' (1982), Duran's sound and image were much more polished and recognisable.

John Taylor, in his memoir *In The Pleasure Groove*, recalled the band's musicianship on Rio with high regards stating: "Every one of us is performing ... at the absolute peak of our talents."

The album's title single, with its classic video filmed on a yacht in Antigua, hit No.9. 'Rio' introduced their famed exotic filming locations and delivered two more top ten hits with 'Hungry Like The Wolf' (No.5) and 'Save A Prayer' (No.2), both with lavish travelogue videos filmed in Sri Lanka.

Video stars

MTV was launched in 1981 and the 80s was the decade of the video stars. Duran Duran were in tune with this and the exposure from TV became the launch-pad to global domination.

In 1983 they scored their first No.1 in the UK with the stand-alone single 'Is There Something I Should Know?'

The press were by now lapping up the successes and excesses of the band, even dubbing them The Fab Five, a nod to The Fab Four moniker of The Beatles.

The glory they had hungered for was quickly upon them, even conquering America too, and everywhere they went they were mobbed by the baying crowds of screaming fans.

With pressure on to record a third album (and intending to be UK tax exiles after suddenly becoming very rich) they decamped to Cannes, France to record 'Seven and the Ragged Tiger'. The title references the five band members plus the two managers while "the tiger is success".

The LP garnered mixed reviews but three more hit singles were borne from it. 'Union of the Snake' hit No.3, 'New Moon on Monday' got to No.9 while 'The Reflex' (remixed by Chic's Nile Rodgers) scored them their second (and final) UK No.1 but, crucially, their first US No.1.

Now at the peak of their powers, they embarked on their highly successful 1983-4 'Sing Blue Silver' world tour, famously captured in the live album 'Arena' (1984) which also included one extra studio recording – 'Wild Boys', a No.2 UK hit released with the world's most expensive video at that point.

Cracks in the pavement

By 1985, the fame and the fortune and "too many late nights" caught up with the Wild Boys.

Side projects The Power Station (John and Andy with Robert Palmer) and Arcadia (Simon and Nick, partly with Roger) came and went but they got together for the one last single as the original five-piece with Bond theme 'A View To A Kill' (No.2 in UK), produced by another Chic band member, Bernard Edwards.

They also played Live Aid in the US. Their appearance at Philadelphia in front of 90,000 people was to be their last as the classic line-up until their 25th anniversary dates reunited them on stage in 2003. Just don't mention Simon's bum-note on 'A View To A Kill'.

Roger did not want to continue for the time being, feeling exhausted by the five intense years of fame and Andy was non-committal to the next LP's sessions so John, Nick and Simon continued as a three-piece.

The trio teamed up with Nile Rodgers again for what became their next album 'Notorious' (1986) but they had lost their global superstar crown and suddenly found themselves working harder for the hits.

No ordinary comeback

The intervening years may have seen them struggle to score the hits but the 'Wedding Album' (1993) - their highest charting album (No.4) since Seven and the Ragged Tiger - boasted three singles that hit the Top 40 - 'Ordinary World' (No.6), 'Come Undone' (No.13) and 'Too Much Information'. Four singles also charted in the USA.

Duran were back with some mature and timeless classics, and looking as cool as ever. A follow up covers album, 'Thank You' (1995) contained a version of 'Perfect Day' described by Lou Reed himself as the best ever cover version of one of his songs.

With their 11th studio album 'Astronaut' (2004) featuring the original five members recording together for the first time since 'A View to A Kill', the tour that followed gave younger fans who missed their original heyday a chance to see the Fab Five in concert.

They did not disappoint, and filled the world's arenas with their hits all over again. Though Andy Taylor came and went again, John, Nick, Simon and Roger are still very much working together.

Legacy

The success of 'Paper Gods' (2015) which saw them team up with Mark Ronson and Nile Rodgers on the hit single 'Pressure Off' (also featuring Janelle Monae) and subsequent years of touring the album and headlining festivals has spurred them on like The Rolling Stones of New Wave.

A 15th studio album is currently in progress and due to be released later this year.

Wild Boys? Not really theses days, but it was great to meet one of my musical heroes, John Taylor, at a charity ball at Millennium Point in Birmingham in December 2019.

It will see Duran Duran become one of only a handful of artists to release LPs in five different decades.

With a star on the Hollywood (LA) Walk of Fame, three Ivor Novellos, two Grammys and two lifetime achievement awards from

MTV and The Brits respectively, Duran Duran's position in the pantheon of rock 'n' roll establishment is secured.

Not bad for a plan hatched by two buddies from a quiet housing estate in Hollywood, Birmingham.

My top three Duran Duran tracks

1. Rio
2. Ordinary World
3. Hungry Like The Wolf
Underrated track = My Antarctica

• Check out James' 'D is for Duran Duran' Spotify playlist at https://spoti.fi/3ciCVU3

"It was a real labour of love to write about Duran Duran. Their story is legend in Birmingham, particularly to those of us from Hollywood, just like John and Nick.

"They lived out our pop music dreams out for us and most people I speak to from 'round my way' have either an anecdote or a tale to tell about an encounter with a Duran star.

"By the way, did I tell you John Taylor's mum was my dinner lady at Shawhurst Infants School back in the early 80s?!"

"Hey there Mr Blue, we're so pleased with what you do"

'E' is for Electric Light Orchestra

AN UNDERRATED musical genius, a hugely influential producer, Son of The Beatles – just a few ways to describe Jeff Lynne, the main man of Electric Light Orchestra (ELO).

How did they create that famous layered sound and what inspired their most famous song - 'Mr Blue Sky'?

Sound on sound

Born in Shard End, Birmingham in 1947, to parents Nancy and Phillip, Jeff Lynne's first instrument was a guitar his father bought him for £2 and he was still using as recently as 2012!

But it was Lynne's rather expensive purchase of a Bang & Olufsen tape recorder in 1968 that was to ultimately be the genesis of the sound we all instantly recognise him and ELO for today.

Speaking on a BBC radio interview, Lynne explained his father had to sign for the pricey piece of kit that allowed him to keep layering tracks, bouncing from left to right and back again, creating that 'phasing' sound he'd heard on records like 'Itchycoo Park' by The Small Faces.

Costing 120 Guineas (which is about £1,500 in today's money) Lynne described it as a perfect machine that was better than a lot of studio equipment at the time.

"You could layer sound on sound, up to about 15 or so tracks without losing the quality," he said.
"I had to have it 'on the drip' so I paid for it, a fiver a week, from the money I got playing in The Idle Race (a band he was in with Roy Wood before they became The Move)."

He still has the tape recorder and it still works, more than 50 years later.

Lynne has a love of technology and a love of songs, starting them off with chords and later adding tunes and lyrics. It helped him develop the famous sound of ELO, the layered harmonics, gorgeous melodies and spacey effects.

After becoming renowned on the gig circuit, Lynne formed Electric Light Orchestra with Roy Wood and Bev Bevan in Birmingham in 1970 as the three departed The Move.

Their mission statement was to create modern rock and pop with classical overtones.

After Wood departed in 1972, Lynne became the chief song-writer of ELO, also arranging and producing every album.

Joined by keyboardist Richard Tandy, Lynne and Bevan continued as ELO becoming a conquering force in the world's album and single charts.

They charted huge hits with 'Can't Get It Out of My Head' (1974) from fourth album 'Eldorado' breaking the top ten in the US.

'Evil Woman' (1975) was their third top ten in the UK while their sixth album, the platinum selling 'A New World Record', became their first UK top ten in 1976. It featured the hit singles 'Livin' Thing', 'Telephone Line' and 'Rockaria!'

Later successes for ELO include 'The Diary of Horace Wimp', 'Don't Bring Me Down', 'Xanadu' and 'All Over The World'.

Their compilations brim with belters but there's one song in particular they will always be remembered for.

Blue Skies forecast

"Morning! Today's forecast calls for Blue Skies" heralds the radio voice over at the start of 'Mr Blue Sky', undoubtedly ELO's most famous song.

Jeff Lynne came up with this track after he locked himself away in a Swiss chalet attempting to write the follow-up to 'A New World Record'.

Lynne states 'Mr Blue Sky' captured his vision of what ELO was all about. He started with the 'thumping' chords on an electric piano but the sky was foggy. Then, one day, the blue sky returned.

"It was dark and misty for two weeks, and I didn't come up with a thing," Lynne recalled.

"Suddenly the sun shone and it was, 'Wow, look at those beautiful Alps.' "I wrote 'Mr. Blue Sky' and 13 other songs in the next two weeks."

The sessions became the epic double album 'Out of The Blue' that also featured the singles 'Turn to Stone', 'Sweet Talkin' Woman' and 'Wild West Hero', each becoming a hit in the UK.

The band then set out on a nine-month, 92-date world tour, with an enormous set and a hugely expensive space ship stage with fog machines and a laser display.

Bringing back The Beatles

After Bev Bevan left to form ELO II in 1986, Jeff Lynne was soon in demand as a producer.

George Harrison hired Lynne for his 'Cloud Nine' album (1987) which featured the hit 'Got My Mind Set On You', which led to Tom Petty hiring him too, creating classic hits including 'Free Fallin'' and 'Won't Back Down'.

Lynne also worked with his hero Roy Orbison on his comeback with hit singles 'I Drove All Night' and 'You Got It'.

And who can forget the ultimate super-group The Traveling Wilburys which saw Lynne working with Harrison, Bob Dylan, Tom Petty and Orbison on hits 'Handle With Care' and 'End of the Line?'

Into 1994 and Lynne was the man the The Beatles trusted to produce two 'new' singles for their Anthology collection - 'Free as a

Bird' and 'Real Love', which were created from John Lennon's old demo tapes.

It was a moment of both elation and dread for self-confessed Beatles fan Lynne, wanting to get it spot on, but he pulled it off.

In 2014, after years out of the spotlight, Radio DJ Chris Evans persuaded ELO to perform a set at a Children in Need concert.

50,000 tickets sold out in minutes, and the successful show gave Jeff Lynne - who was this year awarded an OBE - the confidence to not only return to touring, but also to recording as ELO, once more teaming up again with Richard Tandy.

Two albums – 'Alone in the Universe' (2015) and 'From Out of Nowhere' (2019) – have since followed, both backed by sold out tours.

In their 70s and 80s heyday some music snobs mocked ELO, but they are back and as popular as ever because their joyous sound and impressive back catalogue have stood the test of time.

My top ELO tracks

1) **Mr Blue Sky**
2) **Livin' Thing**
3) **Turn To Stone**
Underrated track = Birmingham Blues

• **Check out James 'E is for ELO' Spotify playlist at**
https://spoti.fi/2FOEWeJ

Rock artist Jeff Lynne OBE is honoured with the 2,548th star on the Hollywood Walk of Fame. Picture by Featureflash Photo Agency / Shutterstock.com.

"Another Brummie legend for 'E'. Jeff Lynne is a real hero of my hometown, and I have many happy memories of hearing 'Mr Blue Sky' played in its true home of St Andrew's Stadium, B9. KRO."

"Little Lies and Big Love:

Fleetwood Mac's epic story"

'F' is for Fleetwood Mac

OUR grandparents loved them, your parents grew up with them and your kids know their music thanks to countless hopefuls on The Voice.

Fleetwood Mac are a group for all generations whose story is filled with joys and sorrows, drama and fame, straight off the pages of a Hollywood movie script - and they are all still here to tell the tale.

Let's take a look at the commercial success and personal pain that fuelled 'Rumours', one of the greatest albums of all time, that supercharged a decade at the top of their game.

*

BEGINNING life in 1967 as a no-frills Blues band, 'Peter Green's Fleetwood Mac' were so-named following lead guitarist Green's recruitment of Mick Fleetwood on drums and John McVie (nicknamed 'Mac') on bass.

Fleetwood Mac went through many line-up changes in their early years, most importantly the addition of John McVie's girlfriend Christine Perfect (who grew up in Bearwood, Birmingham) as keyboardist who both married John and joined the band to become Christine McVie in 1970.

Their Bluesy sound had already helped them score a UK number one with 'Albatross' in 1968 and two No.2 hits with 'Oh Well' and 'Man of the World' in 1969, but by 1974 they were left with no guitarists or lead vocalist after more departures.

In the first of a series of personal heartaches for the band, Mick Fleetwood's wife Jenny Boyd Fleetwood had admitted to an affair with guitarist Bob Weston in 1973. Weston was fired, Fleetwood could not face finishing the tour, and the group temporarily disbanded.

Deciding to regroup and recruit, Fleetwood was scouting recording studios in LA in 1974 when he was introduced to folk-rock duo Lindsey Buckingham and Stevie Nicks. Buckingham was invited to be their new lead guitarist. He agreed, but only if Nicks could join the band too.

Hit-writing trio

It turned out to be a good deal for the British-American act as the recruitment of Buckingham and Nicks gave them a more pop-rock sound. Their 1975 self-titled album, which features 'Rhiannon' and 'Landslide' (both penned by Nicks), hit the No. 1 spot in the USA.

A significant marker post in the long life of Fleetwood Mac, they now had not one but three brilliant singer-songwriters in their ranks and, in Buckingham, a great producer too. It was all underpinned by the arguably the most famous rhythm section in music, Mick Fleetwood and John McVie.

However, the mainstream success came at a huge personal cost to the band.

Fleetwood Mac perform on NBC's Today Show at Rockefeller Plaza in New York City in 2014. Picture by JStone / Shutterstock.com.

Under mounting pressure to capitalise on the success of 'Fleetwood Mac', by 1976 the band's personal lives seemed to fall apart.

John McVie had struggled with alcohol addiction and, by now, Christine had started an on-the-road affair with the band's lighting director. Meanwhile, Lyndsey Buckingham and Stevie Nicks' relationship was also on the rocks.

Rumours

From the ashes of their love lives came the recording sessions for 'Rumours' (the LP was named after constant press speculation around their personal troubles) which, although fuelled by drugs and alcohol, saw them hit their creative stride.

Christine McVie wrote 'You Make Loving Fun', about her affair, and it became a top-10 hit. Nicks wrote 'Dreams', which cites a break-up with a message of hope, while Buckingham provided 'Go Your Own Way', on a similar, if more direct, theme.

McVie offered some optimism with 'Don't Stop' while 'Songbird', her introspective "prayer for everybody and nobody", became a tour encore and remains one of the most covered songs of all time, especially by contestants on TV talent shows.

The cornerstone of the Grammy-award winning 'Rumours' album though is 'The Chain'.

Spliced together from tapes of rejected or unfinished songs, the five are jointly credited for writing the epic track that starts as a folk-country ballad, then switches to that legendary bass line, before breaking out into a harder rockier sound.

Famously used on Formula 1 TV coverage, it is arguably their most recognisable track. Its lyrics and construction also refer to the band being links of a chain (just about) pulling together.

By the end of the highly-lucrative 'Rumours' tour that followed the critical and commercial success of the album (its sold 40million copies and counting), the McVies were divorced.

But still Fleetwood Mac continued, and more success followed. After the more-experimental double album 'Tusk' (1979) spearheaded by Buckingham, which contained both the hit title song and 'Sara', further successful world tours beckoned. They released the album 'Mirage' in 1982 with the hits 'Gypsy' and 'Can't Go Back'.

After a hiatus, each releasing solo records, 'Tango in the Night' (1987) was the fifth and final studio recording from the classic line-up, and marked the end of their most successful decade (1977 to 1987) that began with the 'Rumours' LP.

Last tango

Starting out as a Lyndsey Buckingham solo record (he also co-produced it), it remains second only to 'Rumours' in terms of commercial success having given us the chart hits 'Big Love' (written by Buckingham) and 'Little Lies' and 'Everywhere' (by Christine McVie and McVie and her then husband Eddy Quintela respectively).

That record was to be their 'last tango' as Buckingham left later that year.

The classic line-up did reunite for Bill Clinton's inauguration in 1993 (Clinton had made 'Don't Stop' his campaign theme song) but between the 1990s and 2014, each of Nicks, Buckingham and Christine McVie had left and re-joined the rollercoaster ride of Fleetwood Mac.

Buckingham quit again in 2018 after a row over touring which forced yet another line-up change. In came Neil Finn of Crowded House fame and Mike Campbell (one of Tom Petty's Heartbreakers) for their 2018-19 tour.

Fleetwood Mac's broad back catalogue of classic songs makes choosing my regular three 'top tracks' a difficult task as they have graced us with so many brilliant songs that are personal to them but relatable to us all.

My top Fleetwood Mac tracks

1. The Chain
2. Go Your Own Way
3. Little Lies
Underrated track = Silver Springs

• **Check out James' Fleetwood Mac playlist on Spotify at https://spoti.fi/33OJ1rz**

"Fleetwood Mac's wide-reaching appeal spans many generations and I truly enjoyed this feature as I finally got to dig into their back story.

"Their legendary tale could certainly make for a biopic film one day!"

"The domino effect: How Genesis toppled the world"

'G' is for Genesis

IN THE beginning, four friends from Charterhouse School formed Genesis who started life in 1967 as a folk band, shifted to prog-rock in the 1970s and then - by the seventh year of that decade - became a three-piece pop group.

Tony Banks, Mike Rutherford and Phil Collins – the longest-lasting and most successful line-up of Genesis – were turning up noses with their middle-of-the-road respectability, partly because their CDs were found in the drop-top sports cars of shiny-suited, sockless yuppies.

But I will argue it is this trio's 'commercial phase' that powered the band to 150million albums sales worldwide and cemented their place as one of the greatest groups ever.

The creation

FOUR school friends - Tony Banks (keyboards), Mike Rutherford (guitars), Peter Gabriel (vocals) and Anthony Phillips (guitars) - created Genesis in 1967 but it was not until 1970 they started to tour professionally.

Phillips left that year and the band recruited Phil Collins on drums and Steve Hackett on guitars.

Famed for Gabriel's theatrical stage presence they released 'Selling England by the Pound' (1973) and concept album 'The Lamb Lies Down on Broadway' in 1974, but Gabriel left Genesis in August 1975 to go solo, feeling restricted by their long touring schedule.

Phil Collins took over as lead singer at a time the band found popularity in the UK and the US. Hackett then left after the album 'A Trick of the Tail' and 'Wind & Wuthering' (both 1976), leaving the classic line-up of Banks, Rutherford and Collins.

Then There Were Three

The next Genesis album 'And Then There Were Three...' produced their first UK top ten and US top 30 single with the gorgeous 'Follow You Follow Me' (1978), and saw the trio strike out on the most successful era of the group, which lasted well in to the 1990s in terms of chart success.

Genesis as a trio disposed of the theatrics and conceptual recordings, in part due to the explosion of punk music, and focused on writing hit songs, trying to depart from the past. The timing was a perfect storm that brought out the best in three very talented musicians.

'Turn It On Again' (1980) (from the LP 'Duke') heralds the first hit of this new era, being made up from parts of each of their unfinished songs. The track boasts a variety of time signatures making it difficult to dance to but it remains a crowd-pleasing favourite, 40 years later.

'Abacab' (1980), a No.9 UK single (from the album of the same name), was formed from parts 'A, B and C' from a group jamming session. It famously features the first use of the gated drum sound (thanks to newly-recruited engineer Hugh Padgham) that also went on to define Collins' solo hits - one of the most instantly recognisable sounds of the 1980s.

'Mama' (1983), about a young man's desire for his favourite prostitute, was the first single from their self-titled album of the same year and remains their biggest UK hit, reaching No.4. The laugh Collins added was inspired by Grandmaster Flash's The Message.

It has a brooding, electronic feel to it, thanks to Rutherford adding a Linn drum machine track.

'That's All' (1983) was the next single and their first to break the US Billboard Top 100, reaching No.6 across the Atlantic. The song sees Genesis embrace simple pop melodies like The Beatles and Collins mimicking the drumming of Ringo Starr.

The brilliant video by director Jim Yukich depicts the band as homeless men attempting to take shelter in a disused factory. Yukich went on to direct many more for Genesis and Collins as a solo artist.

Midas touch

'Invisible Touch' (1986) is the lead-off single from the album of the same name that sparks a roughly six-year period of global chart success with Genesis at the peak of their powers. The LP went on to sell more than 1.2million copies in the UK alone and would cement them in the public psyche forever.

Turning it on again - Genesis have returned, on their 'The Last Domino?' Tour. Picture by Patrick Balls / Martin Griffin.

Collins had been buoyed by the success of his solo album 'No Jacket Required' which became a worldwide hit; Banks had released his

'Soundtracks' album while Rutherford launched his successful spin-off Mike and the Mechanics. The three were in fine creative form.

Borne out of a jamming session, 'Invisible Touch' is a staple of their live set and Collins has since declared it his favourite Genesis track.

Indeed, it was their only US No.1. Ironically it was knocked off the top spot by 'Sledgehammer' by a certain Peter Gabriel.

Four more singles were released from the album and each of them became classic hits. 'In Too Deep' (1986), 'Land of Confusion'

(1986), 'Tonight, Tonight, Tonight' (1987) and 'Throwing It All Away' (1987) all hit the top five of the US Billboard Hot 100 chart.

They were the first group to do this from one album and the first foreign pop act, matching the achievements of Madonna and Michael Jackson in the process.

Dance scene

A hiatus followed the long and successful Invisible Touch tour (which was seen by 3.5million across 112 shows) during which time Collins and Rutherford in particular continued to have solo project success, notably Collins' '...But Seriously' album and Mike and the Mechanics' global No.1 single 'The Living Years'.

Banks and Rutherford expected Collins might not return to Genesis but return he did and, in 1991, they recorded the 'We Can't Dance' album which became their fifth successive No.1 LP in the UK (No.4 in the US).

However, Collins finally quit the group after that tour to focus on his solo career and did not return until their 'Turn It On Again' reunion tour of 2007.

'We Can't Dance' (named in response to the dance music scene that had exploded during their absence) gave us another six singles and yet more commercial success but critics were less praising of the 12-track album.

Hugh Padgham was replaced by Nick Davis at the desk to assist Genesis with production duties. While the singles were perhaps not of the same calibre as those on 'Invisible Touch', it did give us the poignant 'No Son of Mine' (1991), which tackles the abuse of a teenage boy.

'I Can't Dance' (1991) was the next release. Starting out as 'a bit of a joke', as its Bluesy riffs were 'not very Genesis', it gained traction once Banks added keyboard effects, and Collins added lyrics mocking the models in jeans TV ads. Another witty video from Yukich sealed the single's success.

'Hold on My Heart' (1992) could easily have been a Mike and the Mechanics or a Phil Collins solo hit with its beautiful atmospheres and romantic lyrics while 'Jesus He Knows Me' (1992), a satire of televangelism, delivered my favourite Genesis video.

Collins parodies Ernest Angley in another great Jim Yukich video for the latter, while Rutherford and Banks appear as fellow evangelists.

Perhaps Collins' most cynical lyric, it was critical of the hypocrisy of televangelism where viewers were asked to send in money to the 'toll-free number' in return for their salvation from a preacher who claimed to know Jesus!

Sadly, 'Jesus He Knows Me' was to be their last hit single and Collins left the band after the 'We Can't Dance' tour, though Rutherford and Banks did continue, with former Stiltskin frontman Ray Wilson.

Another throw of the dice

Rutherford, Banks and Collins reformed for their 40th anniversary tour in 2007 and they were due to be back again for 2020, with 'The Last Domino?' tour booked for the end of this year, but the global pandemic forced its postponement until April 2021.

Phil Collins' son Nic will pick up the sticks in place of his dad who now suffers from nerve damage which has stopped him from playing the drums ever again.

Announcing the dates on BBC Radio 2, Collins said: "We're all good friends, we're all above grass and... here we are."

My top three Genesis tracks

1) Invisible Touch
2) That's All
3) Follow You Follow Me
Underrated track = Duchess

• Check out James' Genesis playlist on Spotify at https://spoti.fi/32NcUcf

"On another day I could have written about George Michael, Gilbert O'Sullivan or Gloria Gaynor.

"And that just goes to show the wide variety of musical tastes that pop music affords us.

"Eac to their own, but the late 1980s era of Genesis is their best in my opinion."

"Dare to succeed: The synth pop legends in a League of their own"

'H' is for The Human League

FORGED in the shadows of Sheffield's industrial hills in 1977, The Human League will be forever remembered for their 1981 mega hit 'Don't You Want Me'.

However, that No.1 success might never have happened if it hadn't been for a chance encounter following the shock departure of two of the founding members.

Fate really played its part in the rise of these synth pop legends who are so much more than that song, as (spoiler alert) it's not even in my top three Human League tracks.

*

The Human League took their name from one of the sides battling it out on a sci-fi board game of the time, though the futuristic group were formerly called The Future.

Martyn Ware and Ian Marsh had two synthesizers in 1977 but needed a frontman and were aware of Phil Oakey (who had grown up in both Coventry and Solihull) on the local 'scene', who was working as a hospital porter at the time.

By the way, their first choice, Glenn Gregory, was not available but later joined them in Heaven 17.

Ware and Marsh hired Oakey as lead vocalist based on his fashionable reputation, however it soon became apparent that not only did he have a booming baritone, he could also put lyrics to their synth-laden sound that drew influences in everything from Iggy Pop to Kraftwerk.

The Human League embraced the sparseness of punk but did so by channelling the futuristic sounds of electronic drum machines, sequencers and synthesizers, with one eye on 80s fashion.

However, when the first two albums did not achieve the commercial success they craved, Ware and Marsh left on the eve of a 1980 tour.

Nightclubbing

Phil Oakey bought up the band name and though visuals director / occasional keyboardist Philip Adrian Wright was still on board, Oakey was left with no band and it was 'do or die' for Human League.

Next, a pivotal moment occurred. With no preamble, Oakey approached Joanne Catherall and Susan Ann Sulley when he spotted them dancing together on a nightclub dance floor.

Neither had any previous experience of singing or dancing professionally but they agreed to join the tour. Ian Burden joined too, to fill the synth player void.

That tour of 'Oakey and his dancing girls' was not a success as fans had booked to see the former line-up and, with mounting debts, they came under pressure from Virgin Records to gain chart success.

After the minor success of 'Boys and Girls' Oakey and Wright settled down with Burden, Catherall and Sulley to record new material, joined by Jo Callis on guitars.

Then things started to click. 'The Sound of the Crowd' was the first release from the sessions, hitting No. 12 in the UK. 'Love Action (I Believe in Love)' then got to No. 3 and the album 'Dare' that followed went all the way to the top of the album charts in October 1981, eventually going triple-platinum.

'Open Your Heart' had also hit the top ten that month but it was the fourth single off 'Dare', that the group purposely placed last on the second side of the LP, that sparked a huge band vs. record label row.

Most wanted

The band considered 'Don't You Want Me' to be a filler track and begrudgingly allowed it to go out on 7" vinyl - but only if it was accompanied by a poster to appease the fans who they thought would be disappointed!

Not considered to be the 'right representation' of the band – particularly by lead singer Phil Oakey - it caused an internal row when Virgin insisted on releasing it in December 1981, wanting to cash in on the back of the three previous singles' successes.

The Human League - Susan Ann Sulley, Phil Oakey and Joanne Catherall. Picture from The Human League official website.

But 'Don't You Want Me', with its classic video that made them 1980s icons, went to No.1 for five weeks in the UK and became the biggest selling song of the year, paving the way for their long-term success, having also hit No.1 in the US and selling more than 1.5million copies to date.

Their place in the pantheon of pop had been secured, but with a song they never wanted released.

A stereo remixed reissue of 'Being Boiled' (originally released in 1977) – the song that inspired Vince Clarke to form Depeche Mode - followed in 1982, and hit No.6 in the UK.

Buoyed by five hit singles in a row, The Human League romped away with two more classic hits – the confident Motown crossover 'Mirror Man' and '(Keep Feeling) Fascination' that both got to No.2 in 1982 and 1983 respectively, from the stop-gap 'Fascination!' EP.

Perhaps the hits had come too thick and fast for Human League as they were struggling to follow up the success of 'Dare' by the time they went into the studio to record 'Hysteria' (1984) - the name itself referencing the pressure that followed their success.

A raft of producer changes saw the album in the hands of three different deskmen, with Hugh Padgham eventually getting it over the line. Hysteria went to No. 3 in the UK and was certified Gold but had not lived up to the success of 'Dare!'

It did, however, give us three cracking singles with understated love song 'Louise', political chant 'The Lebanon' and 'Life on Your Own'.

Seeking a different route back to the commercial big time, Virgin put the next album in the hands of Janet Jackson production duo Jam & Lewis.

The resulting LP 'Crash' (1986) did bring them their second US No.1 single with the perfect pop hit 'Human' but clashes in the studio with the 'controlling' producers saw Wright and then Burden, later in 1987, both leave.

That was the end of the classic Human League line-up.
Human League did return with the album 'Romantic?' in 1990 which features the brilliant 'Heart Like a Wheel' that is a staple of their live set.

Defiant comeback

But it was in 1995, at the height of Britpop, the trio of Phil Oakey, Joanne Catherall and Susan Ann Sulley, stormed back with the brilliant, defiantly analogue pop album 'Octopus'.

Riding high at No.6 the charts with 'Tell Me When'; 'One Man In My Heart' and 'Filling Up With Heaven' were also strong singles.

'These Are The Days' – every bit as daring and catchy as their early hits and the beautiful 'Housefull of Nothing' could both easily have been singles too, such was the return to their roots and top form of this great LP.

The Human League are still touring today and are a brilliant live band. I caught them at last year's Solihull Summer Fest.

They played all the hits in a crowd-pleasing set that, of course, featured 'Don't You Want Me' and Oakey's superb hit with Giorgio Moroder 'Together In Electric Dreams'.

My top three The Human League tracks

1) Open Your Heart
2) The Sound of the Crowd
3) Tell Me When

Underrated track = These Are The Days

• Check out James' The Human League playlist on Spotify at https://spoti.fi/3cims2a

"The first time I heard The Human League was on a legendary compilation album called 'Chart Hits '81', from which I learned about a lot of bands.

"'Together In Electric Dreams', though not strictly a Human League release, is one of my all-time favourite pop songs, so I was thrilled to hear the group play it live at Solihull Summerfest.

"Though synonymous with the 1980s, 'Octopus' - released at the height of Britpop in 1995 - was a superb LP, and really flew in the face of the trends of the day, which only added to its appeal."

"Life INXS: Aussie rockers truly lived the dream"

'I' is for INXS

FROM dodging the beer bottles in the pubs of Sydney, Australia in the early 80s to playing in front of 74,000 at Wembley stadium in 1991, INXS are a 'real' band who made it to the pinnacle of pop stardom.

According to legend, the group - consisting of brothers Tim, Andrew and Jon Farriss, Garry Gary Beers, Kirk Pengilly and Michael Hutchence - formed the night Elvis died in 1977.

Ten years later and INXS were the biggest band in the world, and they pretty much stayed at the top until tragedy struck in late 1997.

Original kin

Originally called The Farriss Brothers, the band changed their name to INXS in 1979, eventually being signed to WEA after years of persistently touring and recording their own material.

They recorded their eponymous debut album, featuring the early promise of 'Just Keep Walking' in dusk to dawn sessions after sometimes playing two gigs a night.

Andrew Farriss played keyboards and guitar and was the chief composer, with lead singer Michael Hutchence writing lyrics. Tim

Farriss (lead guitar), Garry Gary Beers (bass), Jon Farriss (drums) and Kirk Pengilly (sax and rhythm guitars) completed the line-up of the Aussie legends.

Despite his reputation for being shy, on stage Hutchence developed a persona with all the swagger of Jim Morrison - he even had the same curly locks and leather trousers - that became the focus of the band.

Albums 'Underneath the Colours' (1981), 'Shabooh Shoobah' (1982), 'The Swing' (1984) followed with an exponential level of success and bigger and bigger tours.

After catching the eye of producer Nile Rodgers while on tour in Canada, INXS recorded 'Original Sin' with him for 'The Swing' album, the single version hit No.1 in Australia in 1983 and became an international hit.

However the 'Bible belt' of America took issue with the interracial meaning of the song and record execs wrongly got twitchy so the pressure was really on to come back with a hit.

The band did just that, and in fact they started to really hit the big time with the Chris Thomas-produced 1985 album 'Listen Like Thieves', featuring the US No. 5 hit single 'What You Need'.

It was the first single to feature that famous INXS sound - a radio-friendly formula that was more rock-funk than new wave.

Kicking on

In 1987, the group set about building on their success with the recording of 'Kick' – a deliberate effort to produce an 'album of singles' that would lift them to global superstardom. It worked.

Produced again by Chris Thomas, 'Kick' was recorded in Sydney and Paris, and became INXS' most successful album with worldwide sales of 20million.

That's not surprising, considering it includes a wealth of classic global hits - 'Need You Tonight' (a US No.1 in 1987), 'Devil Inside' (1988), 'New Sensation' (1988) 'Never Tear Us Apart' (1988) and 'Mystify' (1989) – that kept it on the charts for over a year.

'Kick' was the first album written solely by Andrew Farriss and Hutchence and was nearly ready when Thomas asked the pair for a few more songs to really give the album some sheen.

They went to Hong Kong to write, delivering more tunes, but it was in the cab on the way to the airport that Farriss suddenly had an idea for a guitar riff.

Much to the frustration of the waiting taxi driver, he returned to the apartment and put down the riff on to tape for what would become 'Need You Tonight' once Hutchence added the words moments later. Their biggest hit was literally written in minutes!

But the 'Kick' album was in jeopardy when it was presented to record company bosses at Atlantic as they hated it on first listen and offered them $1million to re-record it all.

Sticking to the courage of his convictions, INXS manager Chris Murphy hatched a make-or-break plan to put the band on a US college tour backed up with radio play organised via a clandestine arrangement with the label's promotion team. It paid off and Atlantic scheduled the release for the autumn of 1987.

A major part of the fame that followed was the age of MTV as INXS' videos for the singles from 'Kick' received plenty of screen time.

'Need You Tonight', directed by Richard Lowenstein, features a famous mix of live action and animation created by cutting up and photocopying individual frames before overlaying them on top of the film. It won five MTV video awards and ranks at No.21 in MTV's top 100 greatest videos of all time.

Live fantastic

After touring 'Kick' extensively, INXS released their seventh album 'X' in 1990, marking ten years since their debut LP.

Though not quite as successful as its predecessor, 'X' hit No.2 in the UK album charts on a 44-week run and spawned more hits, namely 'Suicide Blonde' (1990) with its brilliant blues harp motif, 'Disappear' (1990), 'By My Side' (1990) and 'Bitter Tears' (1991).

Hutchence was by now in a relationship with Kylie Minogue and while the romance converted her from a pop pin-up into an international sex symbol, it boosted his popularity, opening up the band to an even wider audience.

Life INXS: Kirk Whitehouse's Smashed Hits Broken Vinyl take on the classic 'Kick' album.

The 'Summer XS Tour' that followed the 'X' album saw them play to 74,000 fans at Wembley stadium on 13 July 1991. Seventeen camera angles captured the spectacle and the London recording became the 'Live Baby Live' album and video, their first live LP.

'Welcome to Wherever You Are', their eighth studio album, soon followed in 1992, taking on a change in sound, in part due to the arrival of grunge and alternative music going mainstream.

The LP went straight to No.1 and featured a 60-piece orchestra sounding triumphant on 'Baby Don't Cry' which followed on from lead-off single 'Heaven Sent' in 1992. 'Taste It' and 'Beautiful Girl' (1993) were also hits on the 2million-selling album.

Fateful incident

Citing the need for a break, INXS did not tour 'Welcome to Wherever You Are'. However, during the European promotion of the album a fateful incident happened that would alter Hutchence's behaviour forever and, some say, eventually contributed to his premature death in 1997.

While on a night out in Copenhagen with supermodel girlfriend Helena Christensen, Hutchence got into a fight with a taxi driver.

He suffered a fractured skull due to a fall, causing a loss of sense of smell and taste. The alleged injury also caused him to act erratically, abusively and to suffer insomnia.

INXS recorded 'Full Moon, Dirty Hearts' in 1993 but during the recording on the Isle of Capri, Hutchence, still struggling from his head injury, became increasingly aggressive towards band members and smashed up the studio, once threatening bass player Garry Beers with a knife.

The album did not live up to the standards of the previous three and in 1994 a Greatest Hits was released.

The group did reconvene for the 1997 LP 'Elegantly Wasted' with a decent single of the same name. The choruses are overdubbed with Hutchence singing "We're better than Oasis" in response to Noel Gallagher rather pathetically calling him a "has-been" at the 1996 Brit Awards.

But personal problems were mounting for Hutchence who was by now in a relationship with Paula Yates.

When Yates, their daughter Heavenly Hiraani Tiger Lily and her daughters with ex-husband Bob Geldof were halted from seeing Hutchence (by a court order) during rehearsals for the 'Elegantly Wasted' he was furious and upset and had already been drinking and taking drugs.

Never Tear Us Apart

Hutchence shocked the whole world when he took his own life in the Ritz Carlton hotel in Sydney on November 22, 1997, aged just 37.

The 'Mystify' documentary of 2019 questioned whether the alleged brain injury suffered after being attacked in 1992 contributed to his depressive state, that was already impacted by the personal turmoil of his turbulent relationship with Yates and drug use.

Revered in life by heavyweight rock contemporaries like Bono and Nick Cave, Cave sang 'Into My Arms' at Hutchence's funeral.

Another legend was gone too soon but his legacy with INXS lives on.

Aussie journalist Andrew Mueller, writing for The Guardian in 2014, said of Hutchence: "He gave Australians something to dream at, which is what people in his line of work are supposed to do."

Co-songwriter, friend and INXS bandmate Andrew Farriss told Australian TV show Sunday Night: "We lost a very talented good friend, one who could be very inciteful, shy, outgoing and funny."

Bassist Garry Beers added: "I'm very proud to have known such a great, humble, wonderful, caring human being."

My top three INXS tracks

1) Never Tear Us Apart
2) Mystify
3) New Sensation

Underrated track = To Look At You

•Check out James' 'I is for INXS' playlist on Spotify at https://spoti.fi/3chyxor

"Happy memories of listening to INXS albums round at my old school pal Nick Thompson's house in the 1990s. (Nick and I would also listen to The Jam's 'Snap' LP - they are next up in the book - as well as U2's 'Under A Blood Red Sky' - see page 173.)

"All the girls at sixth form were madly in love with Michael Hutchence, such was his huge sex appeal.

"Another music legend who died too young. RIP."

"Bitterest pill: The Jam quit at the height of their success"

'J' is for The Jam

THESE three sons of Woking, Surrey, with all the pent-up aggression of punk, rode the crest of the new wave movement, all the while creating their own unique sound, cramming an incredible five studio albums and four No.1 singles into their five-year recording career.

The Jam were frontman and songwriter/guitarist Paul Weller, bass player and backing vocalist Bruce Foxton and drummer Rick Buckler, all former pupils of Sheerwater Secondary School, who formed in 1972 but split up at the peak of their powers, by the end of 1982.

Weller was inspired to start the band after seeing his punk heroes The Clash, but the three-piece 'mod revivalist' group found influences in everything from Northern Soul to 60s Britpop like The Who and The Kinks, and, in turn, inspired the next generation.

Early effervescence

Introduced to the Top of the Pops audience in 1977 performing 'an effervescent 45 called 'In The City' The Jam burst into our living rooms with a whizz and a bang on their first top 40 hit that was typical of the fast-paced punky sound they championed in the beginning.

'Batman Theme' and 'Slow Down' echoed the energy of 'In The City' on the debut album of the same name which also featured the early promise of great songcraft in 'Away From The Numbers'.

Stand-alone single 'All Around The World' was the next release and got to No.13 in the UK charts.

'This Is The Modern World' LP followed in 1977 and got to No. 22 in the album charts with more post-punk songs and another top 40 hit with 'The Modern World'. 'News of The World', a separate single, then got to No. 27 in 1978. Momentum was building.

Never one to stick too long on a specific sound, Weller's songs and The Jam's style developed and progressed with a growing maturity with each of their next three albums, every time adding more and more fans and demonstrating ever more confident song-writing abilities.

Punk was more or less faded away by 1979 and, dressed in their familiar tight black suits and pencil ties with white shirts, The Jam were always in a class of their own anyway.

Weller's incisive lyrics were already conveying the angst of youth and class wars with much greater resonance than the 'spitting mob'.

All Mod Cons

The 'All Mod Cons' album was released in 1978 and really started to see Weller, Foxton and Buckler hit their stride both in their appearance and with top songs that were more Ray Davies than

Me in my The Jam T-shirt at Paul Weller's Warwick Castle gig in July 2014.

Pete Townshend. The LP was a major success and got to No.6 on the charts.

It spawned the double A sided single 'David Watts/ 'A' Bomb in Wardour Street' that hit No. 25 before the classic 'Down in the Tube Station at Midnight' that got to No.15.

Songs like 'It's Too Bad' with its Beatles-esque Rickenbacker chord crescendos and bassline further confirmed the departure from the punk scene into more melodic pop sounds.

The Jam's third album 'Setting Sons' went one better, rising as high as No.4 in the LP chart, and this is the release that truly established them as UK rock stars.

Featuring 'Thick as Thieves', 'Private Hell' and 'Little Boy Soldiers' it was initially planned as a concept album telling the story of three boyhood friends who later reunite as adults after a war.

A prophecy for the band? Weller has consistently ruled out a reunion of The Jam's original trio.

Class hatred

Lyrically, 'Setting Sons' was much more sharp-witted as was captured on the No.3 hit 'The Eton Rifles' (1979) with the brilliant lines: "Sup up your beer and collect your fags, there's a row going on down near Slough."

'The Eton Rifles' recalls a street fight Weller read about in the papers between right-to-work marchers in Slough and Eton College pupils who were jeering them during their lunchbreak. It was typical of the class hatred in Weller's songs of the time.

The fags line is a double entendre meaning 'pick up your cigarettes' as well as referring to the hierarchies of boarding schools where the 'fags' were servants to the older students.

By the start of the 1980s The Jam seemed unstoppable. 'Going Underground/Dreams of Children', another double A side, scored them their first chart topper in March 1980.

They followed this up with 'Start!' which also hit No.1, and famously featured a bassline riff heard on 'Taxman' by The Beatles, as did the brilliant B side 'Liza Radley'.

Start of the end

'Start!' was taken from the 'Sound Affects' album that got to No. 2 in 1980. 'That's Entertainment' was not an official UK release yet import copies alone carried it to No.21 in January 1981 such was the clamour for The Jam's vinyl at the time.

American R 'n' B influences started to creep into their sound, most notably on Buckler's Michael Jackson-esque drumming on 'But I'm Different Now' and Foxton's funky bass playing on 'Pretty Green'.

Perhaps my favourite track on 'Sound Affects' is 'Boy About Town'. It's a joyous two minute slice of harmonic pop, with horns on.

'The Gift' (1982), the band's fifth and final album, was also their only No.1 album. It followed the two standalone singles 'Funeral Pyre' and 'Absolute Beginners' that respectively peaked at No.4 in 1981.

There was a huge appetite for new releases by now and the lead-off single 'Town Called Malice/Precious' went straight to the top of the singles chart and stayed there for three weeks in January/February 1982, denying The Stranglers' 'Golden Brown' pole position.

Written by Weller about The Jam's hometown of Woking, 'Town Called Malice' contains more sharp class commentary with one of my favourite lines: "To either cut down on beer or the kids' new gear it's a big decision in a Town Called Malice."

'Town Called Malice' embraces Weller's love of Motown and features prominent organ motifs throughout.

The lyrics reference the grey commuter town he grew up in with the "echoes of steam trains down the railway tracks" and is said to be a metaphor for his burning desire to get away from the confines of the three-piece line-up of The Jam and broaden his horizons with outside musicians to sate his new found infatuation with soul.

Hard to swallow

That sweet soul sound is evident on the No. 2 hit that followed 'The Bitterest Pill (I Ever Had To Swallow)'.

With a guest vocal from Jennie Matthias of The Belle Stars, it was a real beacon of Weller's next project 'The Style Council' and there was no sugar coating the news that followed – The Jam were to split up at the very pinnacle of their success.

Their final single 'Beat Surrender' again featured prominent female backing vocals (this time from Tracie Young), a horn section and thundering pianos.

It also went straight to No.1. The title is a play on words combining 'Sweet Surrender', a disco hit by Anita Ward, and the military action of 'beating a retreat' – Weller's deliberate way of saying The Jam were over.

A live album 'Dig the New Breed' – featuring some songs recorded at their Bingley Hall gig in Birmingham in 1981 - offered some consolation for fans after they split. The LP entered the chart at No. 2, only being kept off the top by EMI's John Lennon Collection.

Paul Weller went on to form The Style Council before going solo while Bruce Foxton still tours in 'From The Jam', a hugely popular 'tribute' band, which Rick Buckler was also part of initially.

The Jam's influence has lived on in bands that followed - including Oasis, Ocean Colour Scene, Sleaford Mods and a lesser-known university band called Go Bossa (featuring yours truly on organs!) - and their songs still form an important part of Paul Weller's gigs.

My top The Jam tracks

1) **Town Called Malice**
2) **Going Underground**
3) **That's Entertainment**

Underrated track = Tales From The Riverbank

• **Check out James' 'J is for The Jam' playlist on Spotify at https://spoti.fi/3cgNlmX**

"A thousand things I wanna say to you" The Jam's 'In The City' LP, recreated by Kirk Whitehouse / Smashed Hits Broken Vinyl.

"Paul Weller could, of course, have featured with The Style Council or as himself but The Jam's story is such a perfect pop tale.

"They arrived, delivered and left a legacy with all the speed and impact of one of their three minute pop songs."

"The Killers' star is still blazing like a rebel diamond"

'K' is for The Killers

WITH their perfect combination of indie rock 'n' roll, bathed in warm synth sounds, The Killers boast a fully-loaded arsenal of songs that are guaranteed floor-fillers and festival anthems.

Mega hits like 'Mr Brightside' have streamed more than 204million times in the UK alone, while all five of their studio albums to date have hit No.1 in the charts.

Fronted by their very own Las Vegas showman and backed by a drummer I wager is the best in the world, it's no wonder they are one of the biggest bands of the 21st century.

When They Were Young

HAVING been sacked from Utah synth pop trio Blush Response, legend has it The Killers' lead singer and synth player Brandon Flowers had an epiphany after seeing Oasis in concert. Realising he wanted to be in a rock band he responded to a Las Vegas newspaper ad by guitarist Dave Keuning.

They bonded over musical similarities and by November 2001 they had a two-track demo including 'Mr Brightside', the first song the pair wrote together.

Keuning and Flowers were backed by Dell Neal on bass and Matt Norcross on drums before eventually persuading Mark Stoermer to take over on bass guitar and Ronnie Vannucci Jr to be their stickman in 2002. Many witnesses at the time noted Vannucci - who gave the group discipline from the drum kit - and Stoermer, a solid musician, melded them into a great band on the Las Vegas music scene.

The four-piece would work on songs at Vannucci's garage and use the band room at the University of Nevada to practice. During this time the tracks 'Somebody Told Me' and 'Smile Like You Mean It' were born.

The Killers, who took their name from an imaginary group in the video for New Order's single 'Crystal', were catching the attention of A&R men and signed with Lizard King in the UK by 2003.

Hot Fuss

It was Radio 1's Zane Lowe who premiered 'Mr Brightside' that August and the British buzz that followed got them signed to Island Records in the US. They finished recording 'Hot Fuss' in November, sticking to many of the original demos for the album as they had that spark of spontaneity.

The superb singles released from 'Hot Fuss' (2004) - 'Mr Brightside', 'Somebody Told Me', 'All These Things That I've Done' and 'Smile Like You Mean It' – charted respectively enough ('Mr Brightside' was re-released and got to No. 10, after the success of 'Somebody Told Me'), but it was the combined force of all four that saw 'Hot Fuss' eventually reach No.1 in the UK album chart by January 2005.

'Jenny Was A Friend of Mine' was not a single but certainly had the calibre of one, especially given the brilliant bass playing by Stoermer on the critically-acclaimed track while 'Glamorous Indie Rock & Roll' set out The Killers' manifesto for global music domination.

The band embraced the power of the music video with frontman Flowers proving a more than able star turn for the cameras.

The second video for 'Mr Brightside', starring Eric Roberts as a love rival, was a brilliant pastiche of Baz Luhrmann's 'Moulin Rouge!' movie.

Awards from MTV, the NME, Rolling Stone magazine, Grammy nominations and a successful world tour followed, including playing Live 8 in July, and, by the end of 2005, the group secured a powerful mandate from critics and fans.

While Flowers leads from the front with all the swagger of Dave Gahan, let's not forget the great rhythm unit behind him and axeman Keuning of Stoermer and Vannucci.

A scholar of jazz drumming techniques, stickman Vannucci's energetic sixteenths that sizzle and simmer on the hi-hats are a hallmark of The Killers' sound, and, perched on a high stool, his showman playing is major spectacle of the group's live shows.

Success after success

'One of the best albums of the past 20 years' was how Brandon Flowers boldly described their hotly-anticipated follow up LP 'Sam's Town' (2006), which was produced by Alan Moulder, and Flood of U2 and Depeche Mode fame.

'When You Were Young' was the lead-off single and certainly set the stall out that The Killers were not just a one album wonder, peaking at No. 2 in the UK.

The album went five times platinum in the UK with follow-up singles 'Bones' and 'Read My Mind' (which included a remix by Flowers' heroes Pet Shop Boys) also hitting the top 20.

'Sam's Town' won 'Best International Album' at The Brits and the world tour that followed included arenas and Madison Square Garden, before headlining Glastonbury in the summer of 2007.

The Killers' third studio album 'Day & Age' (2008) was produced by Stuart Price.

It was preceded by the No.3 hit single 'Human' with that lyric 'Are we human, or are we dancer?' confusing listeners, despite Flowers explaining it was inspired by a Hunter S. Thompson quote about America being a generation of dancers.

'Spaceman' followed and was a huge radio hit. By the time they toured the LP around the world they were able to sell out a residency at the Royal Albert Hall in July of 2009, which was recorded for a live DVD.

By 2010, after six years on the road and having attained global fame and acclaim, The Killers announced a hiatus.

Brandon Flowers has enjoyed solo success in between working with The Killers on his albums 'Flamingo' (2010) which was a No.1, and included the brilliant 'Crossfire' single.

He also topped the LP charts with 'The Desired Effect' in 2015. That album contained 'Can't Deny My Love' and 'I Can Change', which highlighted his talents away from the group.

Battle ready

The Killers returned with album four 'Battle Born' (2012), which was another No.1 LP and led to their most widespread tour so far, even performing in Russia and China. It culminated in their biggest show yet, playing to 90,000 at Wembley Stadium.

A 'best of' compilation 'Direct Hits' (2013) perfectly captured the radio-friendly accessibility of The Killers and contained two new songs – 'Shot at the Night' and 'Just Another Girl', the latter being one of my favourite singles. The video starred Glee actor Dianna Agron, reprising scenes from the group's famous hit songs.

Bass player Mark Stoermer announced he was taking a break from touring around this time, but would remain part of the band and has since played with them on one-off gigs.

He did however record with them on 2017's Jacknife Lee-produced 'Wonderful Wonderful', their fifth No.1 album in the UK, which was preceded by the globally acclaimed single 'The Man' with a humorous video that sees Brandon Flowers playing all of a gambler, playboy and a karaoke singer, all linked by an obsession with ego and fame.

The Killers: Brandon Flowers, Ronnie Vannucci Jr, Mark Stoermer and Dave Keuning. Picture by Kobby Dagan / Shutterstock.com

Neither Stoermer or guitarist Dave Keuning toured with the group on the following dates but, while the latter is also now on a hiatus, the pair still remain official members of the group.

The Killers have sold more than 28million albums since bursting on to the scene in 2003, performing in more than 50 countries over 17 years.

They are still as popular as ever so it's not surprising they were once again the headline act at Glastonbury last summer, with great cameos from both Johnny Marr and Pet Shop Boys.

The band have also have performed or recorded with everyone from New Order to Mark Knopfler and from Bruce Springsteen to U2.

Indeed promotional single 'Caution' from upcoming sixth studio album 'Imploding the Mirage' features a Lindsey Buckingham guitar solo.

The LP is another highly-anticipated release from The Killers who are now established as one of the biggest bands in the world, guaranteed to fill stadiums and unite the masses at festivals with their anthemic back catalogue of music.

My top The Killers tracks

1) Mr Brightside
2) Human
3) Just Another Girl
Underrated track = The Man

• Check out James' 'K is for The Killers' playlist on Spotify at https://spoti.fi/3ceWRqK

"I was only ever going to write about The Killers here to be honest. Absolutely love them!

"The bright sparks of modern stadium-filling pop and rock, The Killers, particularly Brandon Flowers, still have a bright future ahead, thanks to their unique sound and style that appeals to many and draws influence from so many great contemporaries."

"Imagine: Lennon's sugar-coated sermon to the world"

'L' is for Lennon

ONE of my earliest memories is, unfortunately, the tragic news of John Lennon's assassination in New York on December 8, 1980. I was only four years old but even back then - in a world without satellite rolling coverage or the internet - that dark day was inescapable on the TV, radio and in the newspapers; such was the magnitude of his murder.

The world was robbed of one of the greatest ever songwriters and we still wonder today what music he might have blessed us with if he had been here today or even if The Beatles might have reunited.

Lennon had released 'Double Fantasy' with wife Yoko Ono the month before his death, but it was his seminal song 'Imagine' that went to the top of the charts in the aftermath. The album of the same name, originally released in 1971, is also one of his finest.

Primal scream

'IMAGINE' was John Lennon's second solo album since The Beatles went their separate ways and some of the needle with Paul McCartney is evident in the songs recorded over three months at his home in Tittenhurst Park (Ascot Sound Studios), Abbey Road and the Record Plant in New York City in early to mid-1971.

The Beatles had been plagued by business difficulties after Brian Epstein's death in 1967, eventually all falling behind Allen Klein as manager, much to Paul McCartney's displeasure. Ringo Starr and George Harrison had already briefly left and returned. Lennon quit in September 1969, but it was not clear how long for.

Then, following a row over the release of Paul McCartney's solo album clashing with the scheduling for 'Let It Be' and Starr's debut album, coupled with McCartney's dislike of Phil Spector's treatment of some of the 'Let It Be' tracks (mainly the title track), he officially left the Fab Four on April 10, 1970.

With headlines like "Paul Quits The Beatles" the other three felt betrayed and Lennon certainly used words as weapons on the 'Imagine' album.

After the big split, John Lennon and Yoko Ono had entered a period of four months of 'Primal Therapy' – a therapy promoted by Arthur Janov where the patient recalls and re-enacts disturbing past experiences and expresses normally repressed anger or frustration through spontaneous and unrestrained screams, hysteria, or violence.

Lennon got Janov and his wife in to conduct the therapy after being impressed by a copy of Janov's "The Primal Scream" book that had been posted to him at Tittenhurst.

The therapy influenced debut album 'John Lennon/Plastic Ono Band' and it can still be heard on 'Imagine' which was co-produced by John and Yoko with Phil Spector.

Fellow ex-Beatle George Harrison featured (on half the tracks), along with another Beatles collaborator (creator of the 'Revolver' sleeve art) Klaus Voorman on bass, Nicky Hopkins on piano, and all of Alan White, Jim Keltner and Jim Gordon on drums plus King Curtis on saxophone.

Living life in peace?

'Imagine', the signature track, was written as a plea for world peace, unity and equality. It seeks a form of socialism with one country, one world and one people. "Imagine all the people, living life in peace…it's easy if you try," Lennon wrote, in one of the most quotable song lyrics ever written.

With its more polished sound and subtle strings, Lennon later said he regretted the production of the song stating it was "anti-religious, anti-nationalistic, anti-conventional and anti-capitalist" but, because it was "sugar coated", people accepted it.

His haunting and simplistic piano chords of C, C major 7 then F are one of the most memorable hooks in music.

It remains Lennon's most successful solo song, having sold more than 1.7million copies in the UK alone and been performed or covered by more than 200 artists globally.

And who can forget the dreamy video for 'Imagine' with Lennon sat at his white grand piano in the huge white room at Tittenhurst, light gradually pouring in as Yoko Ono opens the shutters.

Left - John Lennon by Kirk Whitehouse of Smashed Hits/Broken Vinyl.

Below - The John Lennon memorial in New York, USA.

The lyrics to 'Imagine' had partly been inspired by Yoko Ono's 1964 book 'Grapefruit' and also led the cover design for the album. Ono's poem 'Cloud Piece' includes the line "Imagine the clouds, dripping, dig a hole in your garden to put them in."

Lennon later reflected Ono should have had a joint credit for the song. "A lot of it – the lyric and the concept – came from Yoko… it was right out of Grapefruit."

'How Do You Sleep?', however, had a much less peaceful and more spiteful tone. Annoyed by the apparent sledging of Ono and himself on McCartney's album 'Ram', Lennon decided to retaliate in his most notorious swipe at his former song-writing partner.

"Those freaks was right when they said you was dead… The only thing you done was yesterday, and since you've gone you're just another day," Lennon opined in acerbic manner.

Hitting him right where it hurts, he mocked McCartney's most famous song 'Yesterday', and 'Just Another Day', while also referring to great conspiracy theory that he had died in 1966 and been replaced by a look-alike.

To rub salt in the wounds, George Harrison apparently endorsed Lennon's sentiment as he plays slide guitar on the recording, overseen by Phil Spector - the producer who, in McCartney's eyes, ruined 'Let It Be' while Ringo Starr, though not playing, was also present at the session.

Lennon later attempted to dampen the fires of 'How Do You Sleep?' by claiming it was "not about Paul."

"I'm really attacking myself," he said. "But I regret the association, well, what's to regret? He lived through it. The only thing that matters is how he and I feel about these things…Him and me are okay."

Rock 'n' roll

Lennon indulges his love of rock 'n' roll on the album on 'Crippled Inside' and 'It's So Hard'.

'Crippled Inside' opens with guitar picks that you think might will head off 'Across The Universe'. Instead they depart into a bluesy folk-rock featuring piano trills and Harrison's brilliant dobro playing, all topped off by a typically sharp Lennon lyric moralising that the soul within us is more important than our outward appearance.

'It's So Hard' refers to Lennon's struggles with attaining the utopian life he yearns for in 'Imagine'. Another Bluesy number, it stars Jim Gordon from Derek and the Dominos on drums, The Flux Fiddlers on strings and saxophone licks from King Curtis of 'Yakety Yak' fame overdubbed on to it.

'I Don't Wanna Be A Soldier Mama' - another rock 'n' roller - is sparse of lyrics, save to say it lists life roles Lennon doesn't want to sign up to.

It's the only track on the LP that gets the full Phil Spector "Wall of Sound" treatment, increasing the session musicians up to 11 plus the string section to get that expansive feel.

Protest song **'Gimme Some Truth'** opens the B-side of 'Imagine' and had its beginnings during The Beatles' 'Get Back' sessions.

'Truth' sees Lennon revelling in the use of witty wordplay to pour scorn on everyone and anyone from short-sighted hypocrites to pig-headed politicians. It remains one of Lennon's most critically-acclaimed songs, having been covered by scores of artists including, more recently, Pearl Jam and Travis.

One of the best cuts from 'Imagine' is **'Jealous Guy'**, which became one of Lennon's best-known songs and had started out life in India in 1968 as 'Child of Nature'.

Openly addressing his failings as a husband and lover, Lennon lays bare his feelings in this catchy confessional.

Covered by more than 90 artists, Roxy Music recorded it as a tribute to Lennon and it became their only No. 1 in 1981.

Talking of cover versions, it would be near impossible for anyone to recreate the timeless sincerity of **'Oh My Love'** which is a truly wonderful love song (However, Martin L. Gore does a good job of reinventing it as a spaced-out electronic version on his 'Counterfeit 2' LP (2003)).

Which way am I facing?

Struggling to find purpose and meaning with his new-found artistic freedom post The Beatles, Lennon ponders how he might start to move on in **'How?'** - a track that could have featured on Lennon's debut album but instead gets a "candy coating", complete with strings and Nicky Hopkins' broken chord piano reverb style that permeates the whole album.

The 'Imagine' LP closes with the uplifting joy of **'Oh Yoko!'** with Spector on harmonies. Capturing Lennon's 24/7 love for Ono – he calls her name "in the middle of the night" and "in the middle of a bath" - EMI wanted it to be this tribute to Yoko Ono to be released as a single but Lennon refused, feeling it too 'poppy'.

He even calls her name "In the middle of a cloud" and those fluffy white clouds are forming again, just like Ono's 'Cloud Piece' poem which inspired the signature song of the album.

A Number 1 LP across the world on its release in 1971, 'Imagine' is as near as perfect a John Lennon album you will hear.

It captures with brutal honesty his life immediately post-Beatles – the feud with Paul McCartney, his unwavering love for Yoko Ono, protests and political songs, clever wordplay as standard and some good old rock 'n' roll to boot but, above all, it is a set of ten brilliant tunes from a song-writer, activist and musician with something to say.

My top John Lennon 'Imagine' tracks

1. Imagine
2. Jealous Guy
3. Oh My Love
Underrated track = Oh Yoko!

• **Check out James' 'L is for Lennon and my 'Best Of' playlist on Spotify at https://spoti.fi/3kAe3Kl**

Macca's masterpiece marked him out as a solo success

'M' is for McCartney

A TERRIFYING knifepoint robbery where the demo tapes and lyric sheets were stolen, two of the band quitting on the eve of recording, collapsing during the sessions being produced at a sub-standard studio, and a run-in with a hostile political activist.

All of these incidents plagued the creation of Band on the Run, yet Paul McCartney later dismissed the "strength through adversity" theory behind the success of what remains his most acclaimed album outside of The Beatles.

McCartney is right to reflect that while he and what was left of his band Wings 'found themselves in times of trouble' the LP would still have been a critical and commercial hit regardless. Let's take a look at the making of Macca's masterpiece.

*

The year is 1973 and, after the first two albums by Paul McCartney and his new band Wings 'Wild Life' (1971) and 'Red Rose Speedway' (1973) met with varied receptions, he is looking to shake things up and get away from the UK, taking advantage of his label EMI's global presence.

Lagos in Nigeria had an EMI studio (of sorts) and would offer a big change of scenery for Wings' third long player (McCartney's fifth since leaving The Beatles).

Having recently registered an international hit with the James Bond movie theme to 'Live and Let Die' (1973) that had given him a credibility stock rise, he was primed to get back in the studio again.

The single **'Helen Wheels'** - a play on the name of the McCartneys' family Land Rover - immediately preceded the LP but was not originally on the UK release.

Meanwhile, his three former Beatles bandmates were embroiled in a bitter legal battle with the group's former manager Allen Klein - the man whose business dealings led to McCartney formally quitting the band back in 1970, sparking a falling out with John, George and Ringo.

Buoyed by this apparent moral victory and a new-found feeling of creative liberation, there is a definite thread of escape and freedom in the nine songs featured on 'Band on the Run'.

"It's a kind of prison escape," McCartney later told *Melody Maker*. "At the beginning the guy is stuck inside four walls, and eventually breaks out. There is a thread, but it's not a concept album."

However, problems flared up when guitarist Henry McCullough and drummer Denny Seiwell quit Wings before the band had even boarded the plane, leaving Paul and Linda McCartney and guitarist Denny Laine as a three-piece.

The trio pressed ahead, supported by The Beatles' engineer Geoff Emerick, flying out to Africa hoping on a tropical sunny retreat for the daytime and recording sessions by night.

Instead, they landed in a Nigeria gripped by a military dictatorship, poverty and disease. It was also their rainy season.

With no drummer, McCartney played the kit himself, as well as taking on the lead guitar parts, in addition to his usual roles as bass player, pianist and lead vocalist.

To make matters worse, when they got out there they found the studio fell well short of the kind of standards they were used to at the plush surroundings of Abbey Road.

Then, while out walking one evening, Paul and Linda McCartney were robbed at knifepoint, the thieves taking their valuables, together with his lyric sheets and the LP demos.

The demos have never resurfaced (they would likely be worth a fortune now) and were probably erroneously recorded over.

Later on, during a recording session, Paul ended up gasping for air and went outside to try and breathe.

However, the African heat exacerbated his condition and Linda even feared it was a heart attack.

Thankfully it turned out to be a bronchial spasm brought on by too much smoking, but it was a big scare nonetheless.

'Macca' in action. (Copyright free image)

No wonder then that 'Jet', a full-throated rock belter named after one of the McCartney's Labrador puppies, was recorded later, at George Martin's AIR Studios, upon their return!

While in Lagos they were also confronted by Afrobeat legend and political activist Fela Kuit who publicly accused them of ripping off the the indigenous music. Kuit was invited to the studio to hear for himself this was not the case.

The tension of McCartney's time in Nigeria is etched into the opening lines to 'Band On the Run': "Stuck inside these four walls, Sent inside forever, Never seeing no-one nice again..."

Similarly, the line "If we ever get outta here.." could refer to both the local troubles and the final days of the Fab Four. Indeed, McCartney based that lyric on a comment by George Harrison during a lengthy Apple Records meeting.

Later on in the track, McCartney is more hopeful as the song - which is pieced together in sections, not unlike 'A Day in the Life' - hails a liberating crescendo: "The rain exploded with a mighty crash as we fell into the sun."

The title track, like the LP as a whole, begins with a sense of entrapment but heads for freedom, meandering towards liberty.

The escape route takes in the brilliant whimsies of 'Mrs Vandebilt' which was released as a single in some countries and 'Nineteen Hundred and Eighty-Five' which finished the album with a brief reprise of 'Band on the Run'.

'Bluebird' is a romantic calming influence on the opening tensions, while 'Mamunia' adds a chilled-out philosophical groove comparing the rainfall to the cycles of life. Sonically, the latter captures the African atmosphere.

'Let Me Roll It', with its powerful organ chords, heavy reverb vocals and signature guitar riffs is one of McCartney's finest solo tunes and drew comparisons to the sound of John Lennon at the time, wrongly being thought of as a tit-for-tat attack on his old bandmate.

The album was pretty much finished in six weeks, save adding folkey blues chanson 'Picasso's Last Words (Drink to Me)' which was recorded at former Cream drummer Ginger Baker's ARC Studio in Ikeja. Baker also played on the track, which closes out with a slow reprise of 'Jet', fused with itself in another cleverly combined composition.

On returning to the UK they converted the eight track recordings to 16 tracks at George Martin's AIR Studios, adding overdubs too.

Legendary producer Tony Visconti wrote string arrangements for a 60-piece orchestra whose efforts were added to songs such as 'No Words', 'Jet' and the title track, while Howie Casey put saxophone solos on 'Bluebird' and 'Mrs Vandebilt'.

'Band on the Run' helped to mark McCartney out as the most commercially successful of the former Beatles, eventually selling more than 7million copies worldwide.

The LP, powered to the top of the charts thanks to success of the singles 'Jet' and the title track. It got to No.1 in America - where it was certified triple platinum - and the UK where it went platinum and became EMI's best-selling album of the 1970s.

Acclaimed as a masterstroke that embraced a diverse range of great songs, the album was also hailed for its use of the synthesiser as a real instrument rather than a gimmick.

'Band on the Run' was the album fans and critics always hoped McCartney would go on to make post-Beatles and is still today regarded by McCartney himself as his finest solo LP.

My top three Paul McCartney and Wings 'Band on the Run' tracks

1) Band on the Run
2) Jet
3) Let Me Roll It

Underrated track = Picasso's Last Words (Drink To Me)

Check out James' 'M is for McCartney and Wings 'Band on the Run' and 'My Best Of' Spotify playlist on https://spoti.fi/2FC7PL1

"I could not do Lennon for 'L' without writing about McCartney for 'M'.

"The Beatles' main songwriters were just as creative as solo artists, but isn't it a shame they never reunited as a partnership one more time?"

Twelve of the best from the kings of the 12" single

'N' is for New Order

FORMED in 1980 out of the ashes of Joy Division, New Order are an indie band who crossed the rubicon to popular chart success - even reaching the No. 1 spot, with England's 1990 World Cup anthem 'World in Motion'.

One of my favourite groups, their success was once the cash cow of Manchester's infamous Factory Records label and the Hacienda nightclub whose dance music both influenced and was influenced by the band.

New Order are renowned for their uncompromising long mixes of songs, indeed all 7 minutes and 29 seconds of 'Blue Monday' went on to become the biggest selling 12" single of all time.

With that in mind, I took a look at 12 top tracks from the group who are the masters of the 12" record.

*

The New Order line-up today is Bernard Sumner on vocals and lead guitar, Stephen Morris on drums, his wife Gillian Gilbert on keyboards plus Phil Cunningham on guitars and keyboards and Tom Chapman on bass.

The band was originally formed in 1980 by Sumner, bassist Peter Hook (who left in 2007) and Morris after the demise of Joy Division,

New Order as they line up in 2020 - Tom Chapman, Gillian Gilbert, Bernard Sumner, Stephen Morris and Phil Cunningham. Picture by Nick Wilson.

following the suicide of lead singer Ian Curtis. Gillian Gilbert, who was then Morris' girlfriend, joined later that year.

New Order's sound was borne out of the post-punk years, blending electronic and dance music which gave them a wide appeal.

The hallmark punky guitars of Sumner and synths and sequencers of Gilbert are underpinned by Morris' high-energy, hi-hat-driven drumming and Hook's five string bass melodies that are forever etched upon their classic songs.

Despite a couple of hiatuses and some line-up changes, they are still a relevant force four decades later, having released their tenth studio album 'Music Complete' in 2015.

True to their alternative roots, many of New Order's singles never featured on their original LPs, even though several charted well, reaching the UK Top 10 and Top 20, and many even got to No.1 in the Independent Charts.

Here's twelve tracks that trace a journey from their early years in the shadow of Joy Division to their current lofty perch as godfathers of the electronic music scene:-

'Ceremony' (1981) - New Order's first single is a re-recording of the last Joy Division single and is testament to what they were about to achieve until Curtis' death on the eve of their first American tour. Sumner stepped up to take over the lead vocals while Gilbert, who had just joined the band, played guitar. Martin Hannett was again the producer.
Principally built around the chords C major and F major, the song opens with some pretty intense hi-hat sixteenths and tom drums cascading around Peter Hook's bassline that pushes up into the treble clef scale.
It's the classic Joy Division feel but - with Bernard's vocals and a more processed guitar tone - it's lighting the way to the more polished sound we know as New Order.

'Temptation' (1982) - Fading in with its famous "ooh oohs" and some chaotic guitaring layered over a sequencer and electronic drums, 'Temptation' marks that transition to the more electronic vibe of New Order.

Sumner's vocals sound more confident, though this is achieved with heavy effects.

"Oh you've got green eyes, oh you've got blue eyes, oh you've got grey eyes," is a memorable lyric that shows a reticent tiptoeing into the romantic side of songwriting and most of us remember the song being used well in the post-clubbing sex scene from Danny Boyle's 1996 film 'Trainspotting'.

'Blue Monday' (1983) - The greatest selling 12" of all time, has notched up some 3million global record sales and it truly changed the direction of not just New Order but also brought dance music to the indie/rock scene in an era-defining way.

From the famous semi-quaver kick drum Oberheim drum machine intro to synth bassline, programmed on a home-made sequencer by Sumner, and Hook's bass guitar lead to Gilbert's manic synth stabs, 'Blue Monday' is both a club and pop chart classic that has been re-released a few times since.

The original release did lose money though as the intricate sleeve design, featuring a 5 1/4 floppy disk, was so costly to produce and they simply didn't expect it to be such a global hit.

'Thieves Like Us' (1984) - Taking its name from the 1974 film of the same name, the group's dance floor dalliances led them to co-write and produce with the legendary New York house maestro Arthur Baker.

Despite the house music associations though, 'Thieves Like Us' is a more serene affair - a love song with lots of orchestra synth samples and catchy instrumental sections which meant it was often used for incidental music on 1980s TV shows.

'The Perfect Kiss' (1985) - The perfect New Order track? Lyrics of love and death that are more poetry than any tangible tale, Hooky's trademark basslines, computer-driven sequences, sweeping synth chords, and a high energy beat make this a star turn in the New Order back catalogue.

The lyric "Pretending not to see his gun, I said 'let's go out and have some fun'" sounds typical of the devil-may-care party animal attitude of the group at the time.

'Bizarre Love Triangle' (1986) - The Shep Pettibone 12" remix of 'BLT' is so good the band have based their live versions on it since 1998.

Utilising the Fairlight sampler system for the orchestra hits and as a sequencer for the whole song, the track explodes into life with earnest enthusiasm in the lyrics: "Every time I think of you, I feel a shot right through with a bolt of blue".

With a great chord progression, multiple gorgeous layers of computer-programmed arpeggios and orchestra samples and even a vocoder part, it's a synth-pop opera and a nailed-on classic.

'True Faith' (1987) - Co-written and co-produced with Stephen Hague, who had contemporaneously been enjoying chart success with Pet Shop Boys, 'True Faith' was quite rightly a big commercial hit that got to No.4 in the UK in the summer of 1987, and preceded the hugely popular 'Substance' compilation album.

One of their best songs thanks to its catchy hooks and Sumner's reflective words, it is backed by another corker in '1963' that, in a parallel universe, is surely the 'A side'. Both songs were borne out of a 10-day writing and recording session with Hague that can only be reviewed as a week and a half well spent.

The accompanying surreal music video with two men slapping each other in time to the beat is almost as memorable as the song itself.

'Vanishing Point' (1989) - There's so many great tracks on 'Technique', the Ballearic-influenced masterpiece that is also my favourite New Order LP, and this one should have been a single, being just as catchy as from 'Fine Time' and 'Round and Round'. Steeped in the hedonism of Ibiza's acid house and ecstasy scene, Sumner strikes a somber tone in the lines: "My life ain't no holiday, I've been through the point of no return" achieving the duality of an upbeat euphoric tune with a cautionary lyric.

'Regret' (1993) - New Order's first single after the collapse of Factory Records was a critical and commercial hit, reaching No. 4 in the UK, and followed their No. 1 hit with the England football team in 1990. Another collaboration with Stephen Hague, it was a powerful return to the charts for the group, and who can forget that Top of the Pops video filmed at Venice Beach with the stars of Baywatch?!

'Crystal' (2001) - Arguably their best single since 'True Faith', 'Crystal' saw an older and wiser New Order swagger into the new millennium with purpose and musical authority, reaching No.8 in the UK singles chart.
It remains a live favourite and the fictional band in the video for the single were called 'The Killers', inspiring the real band to use the same name.

'Krafty' (2005) - With a nod to Kraftwerk in the title and in the sonics, this is an upbeat belter that heralded the new album 'Waiting for the Sirens' Call'.
It contains a simply sublime post-chorus chord change and Stephen Morris' drumming is particularly strong, driving the whole epic track along.

'Superheated' (2015) - A duet with New Order superfan Brandon Flowers, this gorgeous, uplifting and unashamed slice of pure pop is a joy to listen to and only just pips 'Tutti Frutti' and 'Restless' from the brilliant 'Music Complete' album on to the list for me. More of the same please.

• Check out James' New Order playlist on Spotify at https://spoti.fi/3iPaCPp

My copy of True Faith / 1963 12" single by New Order. The artwork is by Peter Saville.

"Another 'shoe-in' choice for me. New Order are a permanent fixture of my top 5 bands of all time."
"When I posted about this feature, I'm pleased to report Stephen Morris liked my tweet!"

112

The story of Morning Glory, Oasis' seminal album

'O' is for Oasis

IT'S Monday, October 2, 1995 and, on my way home from my morning politics lecture at Staffordshire University, I join the queue outside Woolworths in Stoke-upon-Trent to get my copy of Oasis' '(What's The Story) Morning Glory?'

After a wait of half an hour or so I snap up the cassette version of the album as, being a hard-up student, I couldn't stretch to the CD (we didn't have a CD player in our house anyway!)

We'd all loved 'Definitely Maybe' and the singles 'Some Might Say' and 'Roll With It', so it was with great anticipation I loaded the tape into my Walkman. I swagger home, realising this is a seminal moment in pop music history.

*

PROBABLY the best three years of my life, I'd often find myself "standing at the station, in need of education, in the rain" while waiting at New Street to get the Manchester Picadilly service on a Sunday evening.

I never quite stayed on track long enough to reach the Mecca of music that is Manchester (though I did have a girlfriend from Levenshulme!)

I alighted instead at Stoke, where I had made my university home between 1994 and 1997.

And boy, what a time to be alive. Not just to witness the Britpop music scene that was exploding but also, as a student, getting the time to fully appreciate this cultural phenomenon that had a profound effect on me and my generation.

My student mates and I missed Oasis playing at The Wheatsheaf in Stoke by a few months, having arrived in September '94, but duly went to see Supergrass and The Bluetones that October.

Blur, Pulp, Gene, Suede, Ocean Colour Scene, The Verve, The Charlatans, Elastica, Sleeper and even Menswear were also on our radar, to name but a handful.

So many top bands and so many albums to explore but '(What's The Story) Morning Glory?' - which is rapidly approaching its 25th anniversary - was one of the best.

Following Oasis' massive debut 'Definitely Maybe' (1994) was no easy task for siblings Liam and Noel Gallagher (vocals and guitar/vocals respectively), Paul 'Guigsy' McGuigan on bass, Paul 'Bonehead' Arthurs on rhythm guitar and drummer Alan White, who replaced Tony McCarroll.

'Maybe' was packed full of Noel's era-defining songs that could all have been singles, not to mention the B-sides such as 'Half the World Away' being top drawer.

The five singles 'Supersonic', 'Shakermaker, 'Live Forever', 'Cigarettes & Alcohol', 'Rock 'n' Roll Star' became anthems of the working classes and all aspiring rock stars.

Wibbling rivalry - The Gallagher brothers, as captured by Kirk Whitehouse - Smashed Hits/Broken Vinyl.

They were a tough act to follow but songwriter Noel Gallagher's rich and fruitful creative streak that had seen Oasis becoming the band of the moment was continuing at an incredible pace.

Indeed, 'Morning Glory', which was recorded in just 15 days at Rockfield Studios in Wales with Owen Morris (again) as co-producer to Noel Gallagher, eventually delivered some even bigger hit singles and a host of cracking B-sides too.

Their second No.1 LP had been preceded by the stand-alone 1994 Christmas single 'Whatever' - their first to feature strings and first to break the top five of the UK singles chart, peaking at No.3.

Then **'Some Might Say'** finally delivered their first No.1 single in the UK in April 1995.

Backed by not one but two amazing B-sides in 'Talk Tonight' and 'Acquiesce', 'Some Might Say' was the first release to come from 'Morning Glory' and, according to Noel, it defined everything Oasis was about.

The fact they could expend two killer tracks on the reverse of the single not only showed the confidence of the band at the time, but also built expectations as to what was to come on album two.

'Roll With It', backed by another top B-side in 'Rockin' Chair' followed that August and it too could have been No.1 if it hadn't been pipped at the post by Blur's 'Country House' in the famous "Battle of Britpop."

Noel later reflected on the chart race on Dermot O'Leary's Reel Stories, describing both songs as "shit". He felt a battle between 'Cigarettes & Alcohol' and Blur's 'Girls & Boys' would have had greater merit!

Many noted though that while Blur won the battle, Oasis 'won the war' as their commercial success far surpassed Blur's in the months that followed.

Oasis played back-to-back shows at Earls Court in November 1995 and arguably hit peak popularity after this LP.

They played their first headline open air shows at Maine Road - home of their beloved Manchester City FC - for two nights in April '96.

Then, two legendary concerts at Knebworth on August 10 and 11 were each performed to an audience of 125,000 people. 2.5million people applied for tickets, meaning the possibility of 20 sold out nights, which is still a British record.

The titular track **'Morning Glory'** was not a UK single release but received enough radio play in September 1995 to stoke the fires of anticipation in the music world.

With helicopters hovering above a heavy wall of sound, guitars wail, and, with a trademark snarl, Liam belts out the opening line's drugs reference: "All your dreams are made, when you're chained to the mirror and the razor blade."

The album opens though with **'Hello'**, a glam-rock esque stomp, that announces their return with the lyric "Hello, hello, it's good to be back." We welcomed them with open arms.

'Hey Now' is the track sounding most like a leftover from 'Definitely Maybe'. But that's no bad thing. Don't let the anthems of 'Morning Glory' overshadow this great song that bridges both albums.

Who doesn't love the infectiously catchy pop of 'She's Electric'?! True to form it seems to borrow from The Beatles.

The lyrics tell a very interesting tale of love, possibly for more than one member of the family.

With **'Wonderwall'** the Burnage boys scored another monster hit which got to No.2 in October 1995, and inspired a generation of young balladeers to pick up an acoustic guitar (not forgetting their capos!)

Denied the No.1 spot by Robson and Jerome (sad but true) the radio play alone of this mega success catapulted Oasis to a new level of global stardom.

'Cast No Shadow', with the Gallaghers' spine-tingling harmonies, is understood to be a tribute to The Verve frontman Richard Ashcroft who was lesser known at the time. Like many of the tracks on the LP it features a string orchestra and Alan White's signature brush-play on the drums.

It also marks a departure from the raw rock 'n' roll of 'Definitely Maybe' to a more mature songcraft and sound.

Noel's first time as lead singer on an Oasis single is on **'Don't Look Back In Anger'** which opens with big piano chords like Lennon's 'Imagine' with a lyrical mash-up on a range of nostalgic themes. This Britpop anthem gave Oasis their second No.1.

The "So Sally can wait..." chorus lyric is always a Hey Jude singalong moment.

So, who is Sally? Noel once said 'Sally Cinnamon' by the Stone Roses was the reason he became a musician so it could be that but he's since commented 'Sally' is a metaphor for a person looking back at their life, feeling no regrets.

Waves lap at the shoreline bringing a sense of calmness to the closing track and timeless classic **'Champagne Supernova'** which features Paul Weller on harmonica and guitar.

"Where were you while we were getting high?" sings Liam, in one of his best vocal performances.

In hindsight the lyric seems to suggest they were already getting reflective about their rock 'n' roll careers, perhaps acknowledging they could not be at the summit of success forever.

Noel Gallagher has since opined that while 'Definitely Maybe' is about the dreaming of being a rock star, 'Morning Glory' is about actually being one.

It remains the only time I ever had to queue to get a record, like many of the 345,000 people who bought it in the first week.

To date, 22million copies have been sold worldwide, making it one of the best-selling hit albums of all time.

It is considered a seminal record of the Britpop era, has won multiple awards and is regularly ranked as one of the best albums of all time.

Will they ever reform? Part of me hopes so, but I'm afraid they'll never truly recapture the swagger and triumphant glory of those early Oasis days.

My top three 'Morning Glory' tracks

1. Champagne Supernova
2. Don't Look Back in Anger
3. Cast No Shadow

Underrated track = Hey Now

• Check out James' 'O is for Oasis' 'Morning Glory' and Best Of' playlist on Amazon Music at https://amzn.to/35RZZrr

"OK, so back in the day I sided with Blur in the 'Battle of Britpop'.

"But the two bands complement each other well in a notable field of brilliant bands that thrived in the mid to late 1990s.

"We were truly lucky to have lived through such exciting times in the pop music world."

Pet Shop Boys: Innovative electronic duo are professors of pop

'P' is for Pet Shop Boys

I WILL always remember the first time I heard 'West End Girls' on the radio in my dad's car when I was nine. I'd never heard anything like it before and instantly wanted to hear it again.

A posh English voice was rapping the verses then singing the chorus in a distinctive style, with that funky synthesizer bass hook underneath.

I made a mental note of the group – Pet Shop Boys. A funny name I thought, but at least that made it easy to remember.

I taped it off the radio the next time I heard it and so began a now 35-year love affair with my favourite pop stars.

*

WEST END Girls had a slow-burning breakthrough into the pop charts for Neil Tennant, a former Smash Hits journalist, and Chris Lowe, a former architecture student, who met in an electronics shop on the Kings Road, London in 1981.

The Stephen Hague-produced version that first hooked me in to their music was released in October 1985 and worked its way up the charts after Christmas - as singles often did in those days - eventually hitting the No.1 spot in the UK and the US by January of 1986.

Having been impressed with the sound of this genre-defying classic, I was delighted when I first saw Pet Shop Boys perform it on Top of the Pops.

Neil, dressed in a long black coat by 'Blitz kid' Stephen Linard, and Chris in a leather bomber jacket and BOY baseball cap refused to enter into the boring-old party atmosphere of the show, preferring instead to cut a more reserved tone.

They appeared vaguely unimpressed with proceedings but I thought it was the coolest and most subversive performance I'd witnessed. Their apparent nonchalance towards being No.1 simply added to the mystique.

'West End Girls' became the first of four No.1s as they became the UK's most successful pop duo with more than 100million record sales. I know this fact well as I run a Facebook fan group proclaiming this achievement with 6,000 members worldwide!

WEG was crowned the greatest No.1 of all time by *The Guardian* this year and heralded the dawn of what Tennant calls their Imperial Phase, during which they topped the charts with 'It's A Sin' (1987), 'Always On My Mind' (1987) and 'Heart' (1988). It's a sin they never had more No.1 hits.

PSB had filled the 'band of the moment' void left behind by the likes of Wham! and Duran Duran in the mid to late 80s pop charts.

So, what is it their winning formula?

It's partly the way Lowe draws you in with a catchy rhythm and warm string chords, while Tennant pins you down and awakens your intellect with his clever observations and smart lyrics, his clear tone engaging but not patronising.

They have also provided the soundtrack to the life and times we have known in each of five decades from the 1980s to the 2020s.

However, their early image and desire to be different from tabloid-friendly pop stars initially led to claims of them being boring.

Of course, they are anything but, and this false charge inspired the title of 1990 hit 'Being Boring' which counters: "We were never being boring."

The epic track, probably my favourite PSB song, has a much more somber tale to tell though.

By the time 1990 had arrived, the music scene had changed, and chart domination was harder to attain for Pet Shop Boys.

The AIDS crisis was now dominating the news but it had already had a significant impact on Neil Tennant's life after losing a friend to the disease. In fact he had been visiting that friend in hospital while PSB were riding high in the charts in the late 80s.

'Being Boring' - a semi-autobiographical masterpiece, beautifully juxtaposes a joyful melody and achingly gorgeous chord changes with a melancholy lyric about the dichotomy of Tennant's success as a pop star while his friend died from AIDS.

**Pet Shop Boys playing one of their ever-popular live concerts.
Picture by Northfoto/Shutterstock.com.**

The heart-rending story captures the hopefulness of leaving for
London "with a haversack and some trepidation" in the 1970s but
concludes that "Some are here and some are missing in the 1990s."

'Being Boring' cleverly condenses decades of a life into a perfect pop
song.

It was inspired by looking back through "a cache of old photos" and
though it is personal to Tennant it manages to feel universal to all.

Despite stalling at No.20 in the singles chart (it was released too close
to the 'Behaviour' album it was also included on, in my opinion), it
remains a huge fan favourite.

Che Guevara and Debussy to a disco beat

Pet Shop Boys have never been shy of a social or political commentary, despite being a 'mainstream' group, and it's one of the reasons I love them.

Songs like 'Opportunities (Let's Make Lots of Money)' (1986) from debut album 'Please' (1986) and 'Rent', 'Shopping', 'King's Cross' and No.2 hit with their heroine Dusty Springfield 'What Have I Done To Deserve This? (all from 1987 album 'Actually') made ironic and cutting references to the mercenary Thatcher government of the day.

"You always wanted a lover, I only wanted a job," Tennant tells his lover in that dazzling duet with Dusty, so apt at the time.

Closer to today's ever-bewildering political landscape, we've had 'I'm With Stupid' (2006) that mocked Blair's lapdog relationship to George W Bush and 'Integral' (2007) - a scathing attack on Labour's ID card plans of the time.

Most recently, on the 'Agenda' EP (2019), 'Give Stupidity A Chance' mocked Donald Trump as well as Michael Gove's "had enough of experts" Brexit comment, while 'On Social Media' acts as an 'unlike' button for our obsession with Facebook, Instagram and Twitter.

No-one can scythe down the politicians or provide such sharp social commentary in a three-minute pop song quite so succinctly as Pet Shop Boys.

It's fair to conclude then that if PSB had a manifesto slogan it may well be "Che Guevara and Debussy to a disco beat", just as they declared on their epic 1988 hit 'Left To My Own Devices', which featured a full orchestra for the first time on one of their tracks.

At eight minutes long, the 'Introspective' (1988) LP version of 'Devices' opens the album and was a Bohemian Rhapsody moment for Tennant and Lowe.

The tension builds as glockenspiels, clarinets, horns and timpanis rumble around, with Sally Bradshaw's haunting soprano soaring above the unfolding drama.

The orchestra eventually crescendos into a climax that prompts a house bass groove and the aforementioned disco beat, building up to a majestic chorus with a euphoric chord progression.

While 'Devices' is an entirely original Tennant/Lowe composition with a classical music overture, they have frequently combined classical music with their own pop sound to good success.

'It Couldn't Happen Here' (1987) is perhaps one of the best examples, though the song nearly never happened at all.

PSB had approached the late legendary composer Ennio Morricone to see if he would work with them.

Morricone's manager sent them a tape of an apparently unfinished song which they liked the chorus of but added Tennant's lyrics instead, also adding a brand new verse of their own.

If memory serves me correctly, Neil announced the song at The Royal Albert Hall by repeating this fact, adding that Morricone himself was not impressed with their finished song, but they stuck by it and were due to record it with an orchestra.

Then, there was a mix-up in booking the orchestra to record the strings (arranged by Angelo Badalamenti of Twin Peak's fame no less) so, with time pressing to finish the recording, a guy called Blue Weaver painstakingly programmed all the parts into a Fairlight CMI for them. There's a YouTube recording of the very same Fairlight programmed tracks which is a great watch by the way.

Incidentally that Albert Hall show remains the only time the track has been heard with a live orchestra, so I was very privileged to be there in April 2017.

Many years later, in 1999, a remastered release of the song 'Forecast' by a band called Blizzard emerged with the same melody and chords in the chorus as 'It Couldn't Happen Here'.

'Forecast' was taken from the soundtrack to the 1983 film 'Le Marginal' which was composed by Morricone and the track is worth a listen if only for comparative purposes.

There are also PSB songs that have employed original classical pieces to good effect like 'Go West' (1993). Though it was not written by them it uses the chords from Pachelbel's *Canon in D*.

'Happiness Is An Option' (1999) is a Tennant/Lowe composition and puts the music from Rachmaninoff's 1915 work *Vocalise* behind the verses, while 'All Over The World' (2009) includes the march from Tchaikovsky's *The Nutcracker*.

'Hold On' (2012) uses Handel's *Eternal Source of Light Divine*, from his 1713 work *Birthday Ode for Queen Anne* while 'Love Is A Bourgeois Construct' (2013) uses Michael Nyman's *Chasing Sheep Is Best Left to Shepherds* from the 1982 film *The Draughtsman's Contract* which is itself based on Henry Purcell's 1691 opera *King Arthur*.

Some of my Pet Shop Boys 12" vinyl, LPs, sheet music and CDs from the Behaviour era, 1990-1991.

Two tracks from 2016 album 'Super' also use classical compositions if only for the chord structure. 'The Dictator Decides' verses are based on eight bars of Vivaldi's *Introduzioni al Miserere - Filiae Maestae Jerusalem* while 'Twenty-something' returns to Purcell's King Arthur opera, this time to borrow the chords of *The Cold Song* for its verses.

Pop Art

Image and styling have always been a key element to Pet Shop Boys' presentation. Chris usually dresses 'street' in designer labels - most famously his disguise of a baseball cap and sunglasses - while Neil is more sharp-suited and understated.

But it was Neil's Smash Hits photographer friend, the late Eric Watson, who was responsible for framing so many classic images of Pet Shop Boys.

Since Watson first captured them so memorably for West End Girls (he also directed the legendary video where they march to the beat across London), he went on to take some of their most iconic pictures including the 'It's A Sin' and 'Behaviour' cover shots.

Watson's imagery has always been perfectly complemented by designer Mark Farrow's minimalist and precise album sleeves that have defined the "brand".

Farrow is to Pet Shop Boys what Peter Saville is to New Order or Anton Corbijn to Depeche Mode.

All PSB albums have one-word titles too, adhering to that minimalistic mantra.

The sleeve for 'Actually' with Neil yawning on it was simplistic but unforgettable and is one of the most parodied album sleeves of all time. Their signed 11-record limited edition vinyl collection for 'Yes' (valued at more than £7,000), is ranked as one of the most collectible records on the market, such is its aesthetic appeal.

Talking of collectibles, in 2006, Pet Shop Boys published a 336-page hardcover book called Catalogue showcasing their artwork, design and music, and every year Petheads eagerly await the latest 'Annually' book that often comes with a limited edition promo CD of previously unreleased material that nearly always sell out.

Innovators

Pet Shop Boys have regularly set themselves apart from their pop peers by breaking new ground.

After the success of their first two studio albums they were ripe for a world tour, but they decided to make a film instead.

Re-released for the first time on Blu-ray and DVD by the BFI in June, 'It Couldn't Happen Here' (1988) stars Pet Shop Boys alongside Joss Ackland, Gareth Hunt and Barbara Windsor on "an extraordinary adventure from the coast to London, encountering a curious array of eccentric characters along the way."

Pop surrealism meets classic road movie, the film is underpinned with hits including 'West End Girls', 'It's a Sin' and 'Always On My Mind'.

World tours did follow though, and they were worth the wait. Pet Shop Boys created a lavish theatrical spectacle directed by film-maker Derek Jarman on their 'MCMLXXXIX' world tour (1989), and they have since collaborated with the likes of London Olympics ceremony director Es Devlin.

PSB have written and staged a musical called 'Closer To Heaven' (2001) with Jonathan Harvey which even had its own cabaret follow-

up starring Frances Barber reprising her role from the original
musical in one-woman show 'Musik' in 2019.

In 2011 they worked with Sven Helbig, co-founder of the Dresdner
Sinfoniker, and the Wrocław Score Orchestra conducted by
Dominic Wheeler on the score for a ballet based on Hans Christian
Anderson's fairy tale 'The Most Incredible Thing.

Staged at Sadler's Wells Theatre, it was a collaboration with
acclaimed dancer/choreographer Javier De Frutos and British
playwright Matthew Dunster.

Tennant/Lowe - to give them their composers' moniker - penned a
score for Eisenstein's 1925 silent Soviet movie 'Battleship Potemkin'
which they performed alongside a screening of the film in Trafalgar
Square in 2004.

They also composed a Prom called 'A Man from the Future' about
the life of computer inventor and codebreaker Alan Turing (working
with his biographer Andrew Hodges) which was performed featuring
Neil and Chrissie Hynde on vocals with narration from Juliet
Stevenson at The Proms in 2014.

PSB have, unusually for a pop group, also played residencies at The
Savoy (in 1997) and The Royal Opera House in 2016 (which they
repeated in 2018), the latter becoming their 2019 DVD/CD release
'Inner Sanctum'.

They've got it covered

While Tennant and Lowe are justifiably compared to Lennon and
McCartney for their mastery of song-craft, they have a great knack

of making a cover version sound like it was actually their song in the first place.

Damon Albarn once commented how a PSB remix of Blur's biggest hit 'Girls and Boys' made itself sound like the original recording while Blur had done an indie cover of it.

The best example of this - and one of Pet Shop Boys' most famous hits - is a cover version that became Christmas No.1 in 1987.

PSB's disco remake of the Elvis Presley classic 'Always on My Mind' was originally recorded for an ITV Special marking ten years since the King's passing.

Legend has it their pal Janet Street-Porter urged to them to release it as a Christmas single, which they duly did.

With its hi-energy bassline, cowbells and synth brass stabs it's a PSB classic that is often used as a concert finale or encore, such is its popularity and it being so synonymous with them.

'Go West' (1993) is another mega hit that was a cover version. Charting at No.2, it's PSB's take on The Village People classic, complete with a male voice choir for added camp.

'Where The Streets Have No Name (Can't Take My Eyes Off You)' (1991), though, seems to have had a more profound effect in the pop world than either 'Go West' or 'Always On My Mind'.

Released as a double A side with 'How Can You Expect To Be Taken Seriously?', it combines a U2 hit with Frankie Valli's 60s hit, though PSB's version take on that part of the mash-up is more in line with the Boystown Gang's 1982 version.

'...Seriously?' pokes fun at the ego of a pop star - "Your supporting every new cause and meeting royalty...Do you think they'll put you in the Rock'n'Roll Hall of Fame?" asks Tennant with a sneer.

But this double A side is a double dig as its partner 'Where The Streets...' apparently forced rock giants U2 to reappraise their sound and image.

Lowe's sequencers and drum machines recreate The Edge's guitar riffs with ease while Tennant casually blends the rock anthem into a camp disco pop song as if to suggest there's little difference between the two genres.

The Edge quipped: "What have I done to deserve this?" upon hearing the cover version.

And, according to Facebook page "Periodic Table of Synthpop", PSB's cover was the "most insidious deconstruction of rock mythology ever."

It notes U2 subsequently transformed themselves through the release of their 'Achtung Baby', 'Zooropa' and 'Pop' albums.

PSB said after: "We did with them what they've done with them before they did it."

However, Tennant later took the chance to smooth things over with Bono at Elton John's pad in the south of France, as you do.

'It's Alright', a cover of Sterling Void's house hit (though with an additional PSB-penned middle eight), was another chart success, reaching No.5 in 1988, but they've delivered many B-sides and album tracks using other artist's songs, from quite a variety of origins.

My favourites are 'Losing My Mind' (1989) which they produced as a single for Liza Minnelli, and was originally in Stephen Sondheim's "Follies" musical; 'The Last To Die' (2013) which is a Bruce Springsteen cover; 'Alone Again Naturally' (2005) - the Gilbert O'Sullivan hit which they recorded with Elton John; 'I Cried For Us' (2010) which was originally released by Rufus Wainwright's mother, the songwriter Kate McGarrigle; and 'I Started A Joke' (2012) which PSB recorded in tribute to late Bee Gee Robin Gibb.

They even released their own version of 'We're The Pet Shop Boys' in 2003, a song originally released by My Robot Friend the year before. Well they had to really, didn't they?

Action versus reaction

Pet Shop Boys admit they tend to react to their most recent album by setting off on a tangent with the next.

For example, the analogue autumnal hues of 'Behaviour' were followed by the digital up-tempo pop of 'Very' (1993) with its famous 'Lego' bobbly orange jewel case housing the huge hits 'Go West' (No. 2 in 1993) and 'Can You Forgive Her?' (No. 7).

Perhaps feeling sidelined by the Britop phenomenon, 'Bilingual' (1996) saw PSB expand to a more global flavour, mainly Latin American, before reacting with the conceptual theme and seedy electronic atmospheres of 'Nightlife' in 1999.

They toured a 'real' live band off the back of their most acoustic sounding album 'Release' in 2002 but got back to a more traditional pop sound, working with Trevor Horn on the more orchestral LP 'Fundamental' in 2006.

Left - Author James Iles at Pet Shop Boys' Inner Sanctum show at The Royal Opera House in Covent Garden on Saturday, July 23rd 2016. (The picture was taken his brother Matthew)

'Yes' (2009), co-produced with the Xenomania team behind the likes of Girls Aloud, saw a big return to pop chart success and it would have hit No.1 if it were not for some major distribution issues.

Kicking off with 'Love Etc' that manages a reference to abstract artist Gerhard Richter it contains another all-time favourite of mine 'The Way It Used To Be'.

An Outstanding Contribution To Music award followed at that year's BRITs ceremony where Pet Shop Boys performed a medley of their hits with cameos from Brandon Flowers and Lady Gaga.

Then came the more serene and sonically uniform LP 'Elysium' (2012) was recorded in LA which is reflected in its warm sound, and features the beautiful lead-off single 'Leaving'.

However, partly responding to one fan wanting "more banging and lasers", they quickly reverted to the electronic dance sound that first delivered Tennant and Lowe success on what became a trilogy of albums with remixer / producer Stuart Price.

'Electric' (2013), Super (2016) and 'Hotshot (2020) have witnessed a significant return to their core sound, and, yes, the lasers and banging were in full force on the spectacular shows that supported 'Electric' and 'Super'.

It's in the music, it's in the song

Tennant and Lowe rank among the most successful and most prolific song-writing duos of all time.

Their 'B-sides' are as highly anticipated as the 'A-sides', which is no surprise as they've written some brilliant 'alternative' tracks, even releasing them on two compilations 'Alternative' (1995) and 'Format' (2012). Time for a third one soon.

Regularly working on new material in their Berlin studio, Tennant and Lowe's success lies in their insatiable desire for music.

They are both students and professors of the art of pop.

They sum this up themselves in their euphoric dance track 'Vocal' (2013) when they state: "It's in the music, it's in the song."

Their peers agree as, beyond their own critical and commercial successes, Pet Shop Boys have been entrusted to write and produce songs for Tina Turner, Shirley Bassey, Kylie Minogue, Dusty Springfield, Morten Harket and Liza Minnelli as well as collaborating with David Bowie, Suede, Phil Oakey, Jean Michel Jarre and Elton John.

Lest we forget they were a key part of the 90s super-group Electronic with Bernard Sumner and Johnny Marr.

PSB were scheduled to be a headliner at this year's 50th anniversary of Glastonbury following their triumphant cameo with The Killers at last summer's headline slot, but the pandemic got in the way.

A greatest hits tour 'Dreamworld' has also been rescheduled for next year due to the Covid-19 crisis.

In the meantime fans were treated to a lockdown version of 'West End Girls' which the duo recorded for an online festival. You can see it here https://bit.ly/3jG87zu.

One thing we Petheads feel will be a positive from the pandemic is it will no doubt have inspired PSB to get writing even more material.

We still can't wait to hear what they will do next, even after all these years.

I think that tells you everything you need to know about this stellar pair - the UK's most successful pop duo.

My top three Pet Shop Boys tracks

1) West End Girls
2) Being Boring
3) It's A Sin

Underrated track = This Used To Be The Future

• Check out James' playlist 'P is for Pet Shop Boys' on Amazon Music at tinyurl.com/y2th9n4s

"My all time favourite group and the reason I still love pop music today.

"One day, I hope to devote an entire book to Pet Shop Boys (and yes, there's definitely no 'the'!)"

Queen: Golden tracks that mark 50 years of rock royalty
'Q' is for Queen

WHEN guitarist Brian May and drummer Roger Taylor needed a new frontman for their band Smile following the departure of Tim Stafell in 1970, they quickly teamed up with a friend of the group called Freddie Bulsara.

Freddie changed his name to Mercury and the band's name to Queen, immediately sprinkling his own flamboyant style over the group. Bassist John Deacon joined soon after and the rest is history.

Fifty years on and this legendary rock band have scored eighteen number one albums, eighteen number one singles, selling more than 170million records in the process - not to mention being inducted into the Rock 'n' Roll Hall of Fame, scooping Ivor Novello gongs and a Brit Award for Outstanding Contribution to British Music.

Let's take a look at ten golden nuggets from Queen who celebrate half a century of rock 'n' roll in 2020.

'Killer Queen' (1974) − Their breakthrough hit, reaching No.2 in the UK and 12 in the US, was perhaps secured by a change in style from the heavier rock of Queen's first two albums.

A Freddie Mercury song, 'Killer Queen' (from 'Sheer Heart Attack' LP) has a real swing to its power pop sound.

Famously telling the tale of a Moet-quaffing call girl, Mercury was saying 'high-class' people could be whores too.

He commented that Noel Coward could have sung the track given its cabaret elements.

Described as the turning point in their career by Brian May, 'Killer Queen' earned Mercury an Ivor Novello award for songwriting.

'Bohemian Rhapsody' (1975) - No Queen countdown, list or compilation is complete without this - their most famous song, which has been re-released many times since hitting No.1 for nine weeks in 1975.

Kenny Everett got this six-minute opera-rock epic the airplay record bosses feared it would not receive upon its release, paving the way for his radio peers to follow suit as it topped the charts.

Recorded at the legendary Rockfield Studios in Wales (it took more than three weeks due to those famous vocal harmony overdubs), the track is made up of the capella intro, followed by the cross-handed confessional piano ballad, May's guitar solo, then the operatic 'Scaramouche' part before the 'Wayne's World' head banging section, and, finally, the "any way the wind blows" outro that gives it a calming send off.

'Bohemian Rhapsody' remains one of the most revered and successful rock songs in history.

It brokered the format of a video being used on Top of the Pops instead of a 'live appearance' by the band as Queen did not want to mime along to such complex vocal harmony sections.

That video has since amassed an amazing 1.2billion YouTube views.

'Somebody To Love' (1976) - Mercury's passionate plea for a soulmate and some soul-searching reached No.2 and was taken from their 'A Day at the Races' album.

More use of clever recording techniques meant Mercury, May and Taylor could layer their vocals repeatedly to give the impression of a 100-piece gospel choir.

Featuring another wonderful guitar solo, it once again highlighted the band's ability to turn their hand to different genre while keeping their own sound intact.

George Michael's brilliant live cover of the song for the Freddie Mercury Tribute Concert in 1992 was also a memorable hit, reaching the top spot as part of the 'Five Live' EP released to benefit the Mercury Phoenix Trust.

'We Are The Champions / We Will Rock You' (1977) -
When Queen played at Stafford's Bingley Hall on the 'A Day at the Races Tour' they did an encore and left the stage, but instead of just keeping clapping, the crowd sang 'You'll Never Walk Alone' to them.

The band then felt inspired to write their own anthem to give something back to the fans so while Mercury wrote the triumphant 'We Are The Champions', May forged the 'stomp, stomp, clap' of 'We Will Rock You' - which were released together as a single, both tracks being taken from the 'News of the World' LP.

Bohemian Rhapsody - Queen pieced together in pieces of broken vinyl by Kirk Whitehouse.

Brian May explained: "We were just completely knocked out and taken aback (*by the Bingley Hall concert*) – it was quite an emotional experience really, and I think these chant things are in some way connected with that."

Both songs have become rock anthems and sporting anthems too, the former being synonymous with crowds celebrating winning the league or a cup final victory.

'Don't Stop Me Now' (1979) - One of my favourite Queen songs, you never cease to be uplifted by its boundless energy.

Mercury's powerful piano playing hurries along the track like a steam train going flat out, pulling along the carriages containing Deacon's bass, May's guitar and Taylor's drum kit behind him.

The speed and direction of the song echo the promiscuous lyrics as Mercury pleads: "Don't stop me now, I'm having such a good time, I'm having a ball."

It is now widely regarded as one of Queen's greatest ever singles though it only got to No.9 upon its original UK release and barely scraped into the US top 100.

'Under Pressure' *(with David Bowie)* **(1981)** - Queen's second No.1 was a collaboration borne out of a jamming session between Bowie and the group, but the song has its roots in an earlier unfinished song called 'Feel Like' by Roger Taylor.

Bowie and Mercury added improvised lyrics which give it that scat music style while Deacon put down the famous bassline. With May contributing too, 'Under Pressure' was a real joint effort from all five.

It still sounds as fresh today and is hailed as one of the greatest rock songs of all time.

'Radio Ga Ga' (1984) - Written by drummer Roger Taylor, the No. 2 success meant all four members of Queen had each written one of their big hits after Deacon's 'Another One Bites The Dust' reached No.7 in 1980.

Embracing synthesizers, samplers and a drum machine, 'Radio Ga Ga' was a comment on the over-commercialism of radio stations, playing too much of the same music by the same bands.

Taylor yearned for the golden age of the wireless before MTV had taken over - days when actors such as Orson Welles ruled the airwaves in plays quoting "through wars of worlds/invaded by Mars".

I'm sure they didn't mind though when their own *Metropolis* film-inspired video enjoyed heavy rotation on the world's music TV channels ensuring its global success.

It became another Queen anthem and was a highlight of their legendary performance at Live Aid the following July where they stole the show.

'I Want To Break Free' (1984) - John Deacon's song was seen as championing the fight against oppression as well as its more literal love theme and was another big hit in the UK (No.3) and across Europe.

The light-hearted video sees the band parody *Coronation Street*, swapping genders with May as Hilda Ogden, Taylor as Suzie Birchall, Mercury as Bet Lynch and Deacon as Ena Sharples. For the record it was Taylor's idea, not Mercury's.

However, while cross-dressing is a popular comedy trope in the UK, American audiences were left confused and it did not perform well stateside, arguably ending their commercial reign in the USA.

'A Kind of Magic' (1986) - Derived from a line from the film *Highlander,* the titular track of the album is based on that movie's soundtrack but it took on a magical theme of its own in the single's famous video release.

Starring Mercury as a magician who transforms his band members from stereotypical tramp characters into their rock personas, cartoon images dance to the beat of the song which were produced by The Walt Disney Company.

It was the first album to be recorded digitally and the last Queen promoted with a tour after Mercury's AIDS diagnosis that year.

'The Show Must Go On' (1991) - It's hard to fathom that this epic track - the final single from the original Queen line-up - that was released just six weeks before Freddie Mercury passed away, only registered at No. 16 in the UK singles chart.

Of course, the public had not officially known his struggle, though there had been tabloid stories questioning his health, given his gaunt appearance in the years before his death.

The dark opening chords were composed by Deacon and Taylor but May is credited for writing the poignant song, helped by Mercury, with the lyrics describing the latter's desire to keep performing despite nearing the end of his life.

May was unsure if Mercury would be able to record the vocals in 1990 when he was very ill but he did, and to great effect.

The video, that had to be made out of a montage of historical clips given Mercury's declining health, was perhaps the biggest foreboding the show would go on but, tragically, without their legendary frontman.

RIP Freddie Mercury - September 5, 1946 to November 24, 1991.

• **Check out James' 'Q is for Queen' playlist featuring these ten golden nuggets and many more on Spotify at https://spoti.fi/35WdJl0**

"Brian May shared this feature on his social media pages and I'm thrilled with the thousands of positive comments it received."

Radiohead: How the epic OK Computer album went on to define an era

'R' is for Radiohead

ONE of the most iconic and innovative bands in the world, Radiohead quickly achieved critical and commercial success in the 1990s with their first two albums 'Pablo Honey' and 'The Bends'.

But it was their third LP 'OK Computer', released in 1997, that thrust them on to the world map with an epoch-defining release that showed this Oxford quintet were light years ahead of the times.

'OK Computer' is widely acclaimed as a landmark record of that decade, it is hailed as one of the best albums in pop music history and a milestone of the Generation X era.

*

Radiohead are Thom Yorke on vocals, guitar and piano, brothers Jonny Greenwood (on lead guitar and keyboards) and Colin Greenwood (on bass), Ed O'Brien on guitar and backing vocals; and Phil Selway on drums.

Since 1994, they've worked with producer Nigel Godrich and artist Stanley Donwood, joining creative forces for an experimental outlook that has been credited for furthering the sound of alternative rock.

Originally performing as 'On a Friday' - as that was the day they rehearsed at Abingdon School where they all attended - the five-piece were taken under the wings of Chris Hufford and Bryce Edge in the late 1980s, becoming part of the shoe-gazing scene with bands like Slowdive and Ride.

The group were offered a deal by Island Records at that time which they rejected, opting to go to university instead.

When EMI finally signed them in 1991, they changed their name to Radiohead at the label's request, taking it from the Talking Heads song 'Radio Head'. Hufford and Edge remain Radiohead's managers today.

After releasing their debut single 'Creep' in 1992, which became a huge hit after their debut LP 'Pablo Honey' (1993), Radiohead ascended the commercial and critical success stakes with their second album 'The Bends' (1995).

'OK Computer' (1997) then sent the band's credibility and the album's listeners into another dimension.

The LP's title is taken from the *Hitchhiker's Guide to the Galaxy* radio series character Zaphod Beeblebrox who says "Okay, computer, I want full manual control now" which the band had been listening to on their 1996 tour bus.

Radiohead in a promotional shot for the expanded re-release of 'OK Computer' in 2017, called 'OKNOTOK'. From left, they are Colin Greenwood, Jonny Greenword, Thom Yorke, Phil Selway and Ed O'Brien.

Thom Yorke also stated the title refers to both embracing the future and being terrified of it at the same time as well as being overwhelmed by the speed of technological advancement that surrounded them.

Produced by the band and Nigel Godrich, the album features the singles 'Paranoid Android', 'Karma Police', 'Lucky' and 'No Surprises'. It is hailed as one of the greatest works of Radiohead's - or any artist's - catalogue.

The foundations of this seminal record began in 1995 when the group recorded **'Lucky'** for the Warchild project's 'Help' album.

In recording 'Lucky' the band enrolled Godrich, who had been an audio engineer on 'The Bends', as a co-producer - with great results.

Influenced by the war in Bosnia, the track was a stand-out feature of the 'Help' charity album (it was even chosen as a promotional single) that also featured contemporaries Oasis, Suede, Pulp and Blur.

The success of that track convinced Radiohead to self-produce their next album with Godrich, and they began working together in early 1996.

Recording took place mainly at at St Catherine's Court, near Bath - a rural mansion owned by the actress Jane Seymour. The group enjoyed the ambiences there, especially the variety of acoustic settings in the different rooms of the house.

Released in May 1997 'OK Computer' is a deep dive into the farthest reaches of dark emotions that jarred against the sunny optimism of Tony Blair's landslide election victory the very same month.

Thom Yorke was inspired to write the lyrics as an observation of the faster speed of the world in the 1990s while the group experimented with song structures, avant-garde and electronic sounds.

Wailing guitars herald the start of the album on **'Airbag'** which simultaneously compete with and complement the programmed feel of Selway's drumming loop and Greenwood's bassline that cuts in and out like a 1970s dub track.

Yorke wrote the lyrics partly as a comment on the false sense of security of modern transport, having been inspired by a magazine article titled '*An airbag saved my life*' while also referencing incarnation theme that were influenced by *'The Tibetan Book of the Dead.'*

Paradoxically, the group are embracing the scope of new technologies for their music while railing against its impact on their everyday lives.

'Paranoid Android' is a four-part, six-minute and 27 seconds epic that scored Radiohead's UK singles peak, hitting the No.3 spot despite its lengthiness and the assumption it was not very radio-friendly. Radio 1 were actually playing it a dozen times a day at one point.

Beginning with acoustic guitars and shakers, Yorke's paranoia fears "What's that?" while "Kicking squealing Gucci little piggy" refers to a bad experience he suffered in an LA bar surrounded by strangers who were high on cocaine.

Two minutes in, and the "Why don't you remember my name?" section delivers a heavy rock feel with nearly a minute of Jonny Greenwood's distorted guitar solo.

The song calms down in the "Rain down" Portishead-esque choral part before a coda on the rockier second returns to close out the track.

It's like a 'Bohemian Rhapsody' for shoe-gazing introverted types and the song name is another title taken from *Hitchhiker's Guide to the Galaxy,* this time referring to Marvin the Paranoid Android.

'Subterranean Homesick Alien' is a title that plays on Bob Dylan's famous 'Subterranean Homesick Blues' song but that's where the similarities end.

The bluesy guitars and dreamy electric piano reverbs soothe the sonics after the intensity of 'Paranoid Android' while the lyrics were inspired by 'Martian poetry' where everyday things and human behaviour are described in a strange way, as if by a visiting Martian who does not understand them.

'Exit Music (For A Film)' is loosely based on 'Romeo & Juliet', the band having been approached to write a song for the end credits of Baz Luhrmann's 1996 film based on the Shakespearean tragedy.

The band also offered up a version of 'Talk Show Host' for the soundtrack, but used this dark and moving track, complete with moody Mellotron choirs, for their own LP.

Ending with the line: "We hope that you choke" after the imaginary couple end up 'in everlasting peace', it pulls no punches.

'Let Down' should have been a single in my opinion and therefore is my "underrated track" for this feature.

It's a beautifully arpeggiated song with Yorke's double-tracked vocals and gorgeous harmonies juxtaposed against his lyrics which are critical of the Generation X tendency towards what he called fake emotions, or emotions for the sake of it.

'**Karma Police'** was a single and hit No.8 in the UK charts and remains an all-time Radiohead favourite. It's theme is based on an in-joke of the group's whereby they feel the "karma police" catch up with everyone eventually. An anthem for workers frustrated by the middle management.

The album sleeve for 'OK Computer', designed by long-time collaborator Stanley Donwood.

'Fitter Happier' uses the Macintosh SimpleText programme (remember that?!) to coin a series of phrases popular in the corporate world of the 1990s.

'Electioneering' is one of the rockiest tracks by Radiohead and one of their most political too. Influenced by the Poll Tax riots and Noam Chomsky's 'Manufacturing Consent', Yorke warns: "I will stop at nothing, when electioneering, I trust I can rely on your vote."

The black and chaotic **'Climbing Up The Walls'** was influenced by Yorke's time as an orderly in a mental health hospital just as care in the community came into force, and serial killers. Say no more.

With a Beach Boys feel, at least sonically speaking, **'No Surprises'** employs glockenspiels and tender harmonies in this bittersweet and messed up nursery rhyme.

The gentle melodies perfectly highlights the darkness of the lyrics wanting to slowly slip away from a life performing "A job that slowly kills you" while calling for the collapse of the government.

It became another classic single, peaking at No. 4 in the UK in January 1998.

'The Tourist' takes the edge off the LP with its slower, more spaced out feel and was written by Jonny Greenwood after watching tourists trying to cram in too much into their travel itinerary.

Yorke pleads with them to "slow down", and it's perhaps a metaphorical message still relevant today as we wrestle with the pace of technology, hurrying along so many aspects of our lives.

'OK Computer' was Radiohead's first number-one UK chart debut, and brought them commercial success around the world, drawing critical comparisons to The Beatles, Pink Floyd and David Bowie as they carried the baton of music pioneers forward.

However, its heavily-marketed promotion later caused the band to rethink the over-commercialism of their releases, which was borne out on future album campaigns.

'OK Computer' had been followed by the year-long 'Against Demons' world tour, including their first Glastonbury headliner in 1997.

Yorke famously fled the stage during that set owing to some technical issues, yet the performance still put them on the higher plane of rock's greatest live acts.

Frazzled by touring and promoting, and the band released their next LP 'Kid A' (2000) on the internet, breaking new ground in the process, but without releasing any promotional singles, and doing the bare minimum of press work.

In 2007, they self-released the 'In Rainbows' album on their website as a pay-what-you-want download.

Rescued from defunct formats, prised from dark cupboards and brought to light after two decades in cold storage an expanded version of 'OK Computer' called 'OKNOTOK' was issued in 2017, some 20 years on from the original 1997 release of 'OK Computer'.

It offered an even deeper take of one of the greatest albums in the galaxy.

My top three Radiohead 'OK Computer' tracks

1) Paranoid Android

2) Karma Police

3) No Surprises

Underrated track = Let Down

• Check out James' 'R is for Radiohead: OK Computer and Best Of' playlist on Spotify at https://spoti.fi/3608LDI

Brothers in art: Sparks are still burning bright into their sixth decade of pop music

'S' is for Sparks

BROTHERS Ronald and Russell Mael have melded their intelligent and sharp lyrics with a smorgasbord of musical styles since they burst on to the pop music scene with 'This Town Ain't Big Enough For Both Of Us' in the 1970s.

Keyboardist and chief songwriter Ronald is famed for his deadpan scowl (and moustache) contrasting with the wide-ranging falsetto vocals and animated antics of younger brother Russell, the lead singer.

Together as Sparks they have fought the zeitgeist for five decades, trading pop conventions for their own unique - but always entertaining - sound that has afforded them high status with connoisseurs of arty pop.

*

TWO pop stars - one stood stony-faced behind an electronic keyboard, while the frontman is left to compensate for their partner's stasis by presenting their songs as flamboyantly as possible.

It's a popular pop formula that worked for Erasure, Soft Cell, Pet Shop Boys and Euryhthmics to name but a few.

157

But Sparks did it first, and, in the process, went on to influence not just the aforementioned synth pop duos, but also an eclectic list featuring the likes of Bjork, New Order, Faith No More, Depeche Mode and even Nirvana.

They even joined forces with Franz Ferdinand, recording an album together under the moniker of FFS (Franz Ferdinand Sparks), in 2015.

Since they started out in the 1970s, Sparks' sound has embraced genres as diverse as glam-rock to synth-pop and new wave, from baroque pop to West Coast, from disco to orchestral, and even vaudeville, along the way.

The constant force underpinning all of these switching styles has been Russell's distinctive vocals teamed with Ronald's rhythmic piano keyboard playing and their intellectual and often acerbic lyrics that give them an instantly recognisable appeal.

Sparks have proved once again they remain at the cutting edge of art pop with 2020 LP - the No.1 independent album chart-topper 'A Steady Drip, Drip, Drip'.

Meanwhile film-maker Edgar Wright, the director of Shaun of the Dead, Ant-Man and Baby Driver, has been entrusted with creating the first ever Sparks documentary movie, also due for release this year, which includes their 2018 concert at the O2 Forum Kentish Town.

And Sparks are the screenwriters and composers for the forthcoming musical film 'Annette', directed by Leos Carax and starring Adam Driver and Marion Cotillard.

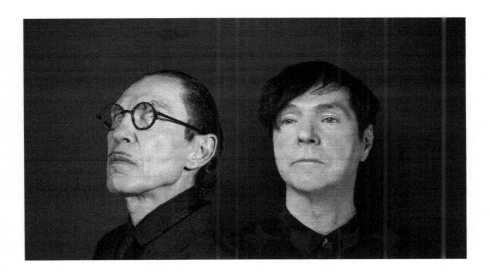

Sparks are LA-based brothers Ronald Mael and Russell Mael. Picture by Anna Webber.

In this feature I take on the unenviable task of talking about ten top tracks to seduce you into falling in love with Sparks - no mean feat given their prolific back catalogue.

'This Town Ain't Big Enough For Both Of Us' (1974) - Setting the benchmark for longer pop song titles later favoured by The Smiths and Pet Shop Boys, 'This Town' hit No. 2 in the UK singles chart for two weeks and was produced by a Brummie, Muff Winwood, who had been in the Spencer Davis Group with his brother Steve in the 1960s.

Perhaps their most famous song, it also outlined their quirky appeal and was taken from the brilliant 1974 LP 'Kimono My House.'

The theme came from an idea to write a whole song based on several movie dialogue cliches but they ended up sticking to just this one, inspired by Westerns, hence the gunshot sounds on the recording.

'Never Turn Your Back On Mother Earth' (1974) - Many people's favourite Sparks song, 'Never Turn...' has been re-recorded and covered by a wide variety of artists including Martin L Gore of Depeche Mode who included it on his 'Counterfeit' EP in 1989.

This gorgeous ode to our natural planetary home was recorded by the "glam rock" era Sparks band for the 1974 'Propaganda' LP, and the single version reached No.13 in the UK charts.

'The Number One Song In Heaven' (1979) - After reaching a crossroads in their career after their two "Westcoast" LPs 'Big Beat' (1976) and 'Introducing Sparks' (1977), the LA duo hired legendary Italian disco producer Giorgio Moroder.

This perfect partnership created their seminal 1979 album 'No.1 in Heaven' from which the single 'The Number One Song in Heaven' (written by Sparks with Moroder) became a No.14 UK chart hit.

Swapping their usual guitar, bass and piano band format for the layered sequencers, synthesizers and classic disco drum sound that Moroder was famed for on hits like 'I Feel Love', Sparks hit on a winning formula that went on to inspire bands that followed.

Stephen Morris and Peter Hook both cited it as a major influence on the sound of Joy Division's 'Love Will Tear Us Apart', and for introducing them to Moroder's production style, which also later inspired New Order.

'Beat The Clock' (1979) - The follow-up single to 'The Number One Song in Heaven', 'Beat The Clock' fared even better, reaching No.10 in the UK charts.

It became one of their classic hits and was later re-recorded for their 1997 'Plagiarism' album that revisited Sparks' popular recording history for a new audience.

'When I'm With You' (1980) - A No.1 hit in France, with the legendary Keith Forsey returning on drums, it's disputed who produced the single - with Harold Faltermeyer and Giorgio Moroder both claiming credit for it as well as the 1980 album 'Terminal Jive' which saw Sparks sashay into the 1980s with a disco vibe, adding more guitars, making it a new wave sound.

It's hard to forget the classic video with Ron as a rather sinister grinning ventriloquist to Russell's singing puppet. Maybe it was the inspiration for the horror movies of James Wan?!

'When Do I Get To Sing "My Way" (1994) - A personal favourite of mine, having loved the CD 'Gratuitous Sax and Senseless Violins' this single was taken from.

It was also the era I first saw Sparks perform live when, together with 27,000 others, I watched them support Blur who were at the peak of their powers when they played Mile End Stadium on June 17, 1995.

Sparks played a popular set that day, and Blur's decision to invite them on the bill was another nod to their influence on latter day bands.

Their performance was as lively and energetic as ever while the album, which was not too dissimilar from Pet Shop Boys in its production (and that's no bad thing), was a welcome return for the Mael brothers after a six-year hiatus since the poorly received 1988 LP 'Interior Design'.

The single hit the UK Top 40 as did the equally brilliant follow-up 'When I Kiss You (I Hear Charlie Parker Playing)'.

'Amateur Hour (feat. Erasure)' (1997) - While the original release of 'Amateur Hour' (taken from the classic album 'Kimono My House') hit No.7 in the UK in 1974, I will go out on a limb here and state I prefer this version which Ron and Russell re-recorded with Erasure for the 1997 Sparks LP 'Plagiarism'.

Giving it a synth-pop makeover, Andy Bell's additional vocals, together with Vince Clarke's trademark 'blip-blop' sequencer-driven production really polishes up and reinvigorates this great pop song.

'Suburban Homeboy' (2003) - Part Rodgers and Hammerstein, part chamber pop, this is a real gem in the vast Sparks back catalogue.

It is included on their 2002 self-proclaimed "career-defining opus" 'Lil' Beethoven' which saw a move away from synth-pop to a more classical-influenced sound.

If Paul McCartney (another major artist they have influenced) had released it it would have been a big hit.

'Hippopotamus' (2017) - Certainly the only track ever to reference not only Hieronymus Bosch and Titus Andronicus but also a Volkswagen '58 Microbus in the same lyrics, 'Hippopotamus' tells the strange tale of objects being discovered in Sparks' LA swimming pool.

The repetition of lines like "How did it get there? How did it get there? I don't know" set to potent pizzicato strings and a breakbeat drum track are both sinister and hypnotic.

It's little wonder this magical song, taken from the No.7 hit album of the same name, places those who have marvelled at its original subject matter and brilliant simplicity under its spell.

'Please Don't F*ck Up My World' (2019) - Preceding their latest critically-acclaimed 24th album 'A Steady Drip, Drip, Drip' (2020) - and the first time they've dropped the 'F bomb' in a song title in nearly half a century of recording - Sparks returned to the pop scene last year with a simple plea to help save the planet.

Majestic and anthemic, a children's choir adds power to this sincere message of hope for the future pleading "Please Don't F*ck Up My World, I'd have nothing to live for" as Sparks strode confidently into their sixth decade of releasing music together.

"Ronald, now 75, and Russell, 71, are back, and 'A Steady Drip, Drip, Drip' shows they are defying their senior years with enough energy, sharp wit and original ideas to continue for many years yet.

"Sparks have never sold out or coasted off the back of their early hits, rather they are always seeking to push boundaries, try new ideas and redefine popular music their own inimitable sound and style."

• Check out James' 'S is for Sparks' playlist on Amazon Music at tinyurl.com/y4omo7uy

Rolling back the years of Tears For Fears

'T' is for Tears For Fears

AFTER starting out as a mod-influenced band called Graduate, Bath's finest pop pairing Roland Orzabal and Curt Smith rode the crest of the new wave synthesizer bands of the early 1980s before branching out into traditional rock and pop, earning international acclaim in the process.

Orzabal and Smith, who share vocal duties while playing guitar and bass respectively, changed their name to Tears For Fears, having been inspired by the primal therapy of psychologist Arthur Janov who famously treated John Lennon and Yoko Ono in the 70s.

Still touring today, with more than 30million worldwide record sales and two UK No.1 albums under their belt, I'll attempt to track the some of the best songs released by Tears For Fears.

*

'Mad World' (1982) - Tears for Fears' first hit spent three weeks at No.3 in the UK singles chart in November 1982 after climbing steadily up the Top 40 following its October release.

Written by Roland Orzabal and sung by Curt Smith, 'Mad World' is one of several tracks which reference Arthur Janov, Orzabal citing a particular interest in the subject of psychology.

While the song is about a depressed young person feeling displaced from the world outside, the line "The dreams in which I'm dying are the best I've ever had" is not about suicide, rather it refers to Janov's notion the more dramatic dreams release the most tension.

It was the first of many hits produced by Chris Hughes, the former Adam and the Ants drummer.

'Mad World' entered an exclusive club of songs that became No.1 hits after being covered by other artists when it became a surprise Christmas chart-topper for Gary Jules in 2003, having previously been featured in the film Donnie Darko in 2001.

That hit did, however, win Orzabal his second Ivor Novello Award (for Best Selling Single of 2003) and reinvigorated the duo's passion for their own band. His first was for Songwriter of the Year in 1986.

'Change' (1983) - Capturing that New Wave feel, 'Change' was again written by Orzabal but sung by Curt Smith and became their second big hit, charting at No.4 in the UK in February 1983.

With frantic arpeggio marimba sounds, Smith's funky bassline and synthesizers layered on top, 'Change' was more akin to their earlier sound, before 'Mad World'.

It was their first single to break the Billboard Hot 100 in the US, doing so in August 1983, and went on to be an international success.

'Pale Shelter' (1983) - Having flopped on its initial release, Tears For Fears made it three top five hits in a row with their second version of 'Pale Shelter', which peaked at No.5 in the UK singles chart.

Tears For Fears - Roland Orzabal and Curt Smith on the cover of the 'Songs From The Big Chair' album.

Another Orzabal song sung by Smith (the pair would often choose Smith for the more melancholy tracks and Orzabal for the ones that needed "belting out"), the title is inspired by Henry Moore's art book of the same.

The song itself deals with the disappointment of a parental relationship.

'Mother's Talk' (1984) - A co-write by Roland Orzabal and keyboard player Ian Stanley, 'Mother's Talk' was the lead-off single for Tears For Fears' seminal second LP 'Songs From The Big Chair' which saw the group deliberately target more commercial success.

Orzabal acknowledges that, although it was not his desire to go this way so overtly, it was at this point that they exploded into the global pop music scene.

'Mother's Talk' is a politically-themed track that cites mothers telling their children not to pull faces ("My features form with a change in the weather") and 'When The Wind Blows' the anti-nuclear cartoon book by Raymond Briggs that later became a TV film.

'Shout' (1984) - The second single from 'Songs From The Big Chair', 'Shout' was a breakthrough moment for Tears For Fears, as it became a huge international hit, peaking at No.4 in January 1985 in the UK but going all the way to the top of the US Billboard Hot 100, staying at No.1 for three weeks.

Orzabal started writing it at home on a small synth and a drum machine, initially creating the "mantra" style chorus of "Shout, Shout, Let it all out.."

He shared his idea with keyboardist Ian Stanley, who has a joint writing credit on the track, and producer Chris Hughes, who both correctly predicted it was destined for global success.

While again being inspired by Arthur Janov's school of Primal Therapy, where people confronted their fears by shouting and screaming, Orzabal pointed out it was about more than just that.

He said the song, being written in the aftermath of the Cold War, was an encouragement to political protest and not just accept the problems thrown at people by government or society.

'Everybody Wants To Rule The World' (1985) - Their signature hit that more than built on the success of 'Shout', 'Rule The World' is one of the most famous pop songs not just of the 1980s, but of all time. It reached No.2 in the UK in 1985.

Chris Hughes' production is magnificent and I for one never tire of hearing it, no matter how much radio play it gets. And boy does it get some, having sold more than 600,000 copies in the UK alone and remaining a staple of classic hits stations.

It may be a surprise therefore to note Hughes says recording the song - that really defined that mid-1980s big studio sound - was an effortless task, being both a simple and easy process.

The lyrics refer to the desire humans have for control and power and look at themes of corruption, which led to it being banned from the radio during the 1990 Gulf War.

'Rule the World' did win the battle for the 1986 Brit Award for Best Single, though.

It was also re-recorded with the words changed to "Run the World" as a 1986 charity single to support Band Aid sister charity Sports Aid. Remember the "I Ran The World" T-shirts?!

'Head Over Heels' (1985) - A joint effort from Curt Smith and Roland Orzabal, this song is a simple romantic affair that goes awry at the end.

The big production and confident piano riffs proudly herald this tale of a man falling head over heels in love with a woman and pleading for her not to break his heart before he threatens he has a gun in his hand!

The band's tenth single, it hit No.12 in the UK and was another track that fared even better in the US, reaching No.3 in the Billboard Hot 100.

'Sowing The Seeds Of Love' (1989) - This epic piece of power pop is often compared to The Beatles but it is a brilliant song in its own right with several great sections that make it so.

The superior sounds of the single highlighted theirs and (newly promoted from engineer) Dave Bascombe's polished co-production plus the great musicianship of the Tears For Fears band.

A worldwide hit, 'Sowing The Seeds Of Love' got to No.5 in the UK, No.1 in Canada and topped the US Billboard Modern Rock Tracks chart.

Tears For Fears had taken their time making the 'Seeds of Love' LP so this track had actually been written by Orzabal and Smith back in 1987 when Thatcher won her third term in office, hence the lyric "Politician granny with your high ideals, have you no idea how the majority feels?"

Orzabal got the title after listening to a radio programme about English folk songs collected by Cecil Sharp, where one of the titles included was 'The Seeds of Love' which Sharp heard being hummed by a gardener named John England. Hence the line "Mr England sowing the seeds of love."

As for those similarities to The Beatles, they have kind of admitted it sounds a lot like 'I Am The Walrus' but in terms of production it is in another dimension.

'Woman In Chains' (1989) - Signs of their maturity thrust to the fore on this incredible duet with the super-talented Oleta Adams, who later scored a huge solo hit with 'Get Here' in 1991.

Adams had unwittingly inspired the duo who saw her perform in Kansas City when they were also touring.

Her performance made them go back to the drawing board, wanting to swap the complicated machinery they had employed so well in the first half of the 80s for more real instruments and real soulful vocals.

So she was a clear favourite to join them on 'Woman In Chains', which is about the oppression of women and the repression of the female soul within men.

Relying as usual on guest musicians, Orzabal and Smith got Phil Collins in to drum on the track, having wanted "Phil Collins-sounding" drums on it!

'Break It Down Again' (1993) - Curt Smith and Roland Orzabal had an acrimonious split following the success of 'Seeds Of Love' but Orzabal continued under the Tears For Fears moniker.

'Break It Down Again' was the first single from 1993 album 'Elemental' and the first newly-recorded single release without Smith being in the band.

It became another international hit, reaching No. 20 in the UK and No.25 in the US, and the top 40 in several other countries.

Opening with brass chords based on a progression I think are not unlike 'Fool On The Hill' the song changes tack to showcase a typically powerful Roland Orzabal vocal and a great jamming-style performance.

He was joined on the session by peripheral Tears For Fears band members Alan Griffiths and Gail Ann Dorsey, who is also famous for being David Bowie's bass player/backing singer.

'Closest Thing To Heaven' (2005) - Smith and Orzabal were reunited in 2000 and, by 2004, had released their comeback album 'Everybody Loves A Happy Ending'.

'Closest Thing To Heaven' was the first single to feature the original duo since 1990 and became Tears for Fears' first UK top 40 hit since 'Raoul and the Kings of Spain' in 1995, reaching No.40 on the UK singles chart.

'Stay' (2017) - This is a real gem in the vast Tears For Fears back catalogue.

You could be forgiven for thinking it was the late great George Michael singing on this beautiful and poignant song (one of two new tracks added to their 2017 greatest hits collection 'Rule The World'), such is the calibre of the lead vocal.

However this gorgeous song was sung and written by Curt Smith, who stated to *Billboard* magazine it is about "having to give up something that you are loath to give up, but only because of the history. Say if there's a marriage that was going horribly wrong but you invested 20 years in them, it's hard to give up."

Hence the chorus lyrics are "Stay, don't stay, go, don't go."

It's a great song to sign off this retrospective of the brilliant career of one of the best British bands of the past four decades who ruled the world in their heyday and have quietly cast a shadow over the pop music sounds of today.

Not a bad cultural achievement for a band started by a couple of schoolmates from Bath.

• Check out James' 'T is for Tears For Fears' playlist on Amazon Music at rb.gy/7v2en9

"Don't just take my word for it. Know that Lorde recorded a haunting cover of 'Everybody Wants To Rule The World' for the soundtrack of 'The Hunger Games – Catching Fire', and Tears For Fears now use her version as the intro music to their live shows.

"Kanye West based 'The Coldest Winter' from his hit album '808s & Heartbreak' on 'Memories Fade', The Weeknd infused 'Pale Shelter' into Starboy's 'Secrets', David Guetta sampled 'Change' for 'Always' and Drake utilised 'Ideas as Opiates' as the foundation for 'Lust For Life'.

"Ally Brooke Hernandez and Adam Lambert have also followed Gary Jules in releasing popular covers of 'Mad World' while Disturbed has recorded 'Shout'."

Attention please for U2's Achtung Baby - the Irish rockers' revolutionary recording

'U' is for U2

IRISH rockers U2 are truly one of the greatest bands of all time and a massive global brand, so it's easy to forget it's their talent as musicians and songwriters that has put them at the pinnacle of popular music.

Such is their commercial power, the Dublin four-piece placed third in *The Sunday Times Musicians Rich List of 2019*, with an estimated wealth of £583million, beaten only by Andrew Lloyd-Webber and Paul McCartney.

No surprise as they have released 14 studio albums and have sold an estimated 170 million records worldwide, scooping 22 Grammy Awards (that's more than any other band) and, in 2005, were inducted into the Rock and Roll Hall of Fame at the first time of asking.

They initially found huge success in the 1980s, particularly with 'The Joshua Tree' and 'Rattle and Hum' LPs, but here's why I think 1991's 'Achtung Baby' is their best album.

*

Four teenagers from Mount Temple Comprehensive in Dublin - Paul Hewson AKA Bono (lead vocals and rhythm guitar), Dave Evans AKA the Edge (lead guitar, keyboards, and backing vocals),

Adam Clayton (bass guitar) and Larry Mullen Jr. (drums and percussion) - first formed the band in 1976.

They were originally called Feedback, before changing to The Hype in 1977, and finally settling on U2 - the name of an American cold war spy-plane.

Four years after they started out, they had a recording deal with Island Records from where they went on to conquer the world throughout the 1980s with their post-punk songs and sociopolitical themes, earning critical acclaim along the way.

U2's third album 'War' got to No.1 in the UK album charts, knocking Michael Jackson's thriller off top spot, also getting to No.12 and going 'Gold' in the US.

My first real experience of properly listening to U2 comes in here too - spinning their 'Under A Blood Red Sky' (1984) LP (No.2 in the UK) on the decks at my mate Nick's house when we were teenagers.

I was never really a rock music fan beforehand, but there was something about the musicianship and skill on this live recording of the show at the Red Rocks Amphitheatre on June 5, 1983 that inspired me to follow.

The atmosphere of U2 playing songs like 'October', 'New Year's Day', 'I Will Follow' and Bono introducing 'Sunday Bloody Sunday' with the words: "This is song is not a rebel song" sent shivers down my spine as if I were at the concert in person.

Revolutionary record - The album sleeve to U2's 1991 seminal LP 'Achtung Baby' - which was designed by Steve Avrill and Shaughn McGrath - abandoned the regular 'heroic' landscape shots of the band for a patchwork of snapshot images, and more colour.

U2 followed up with 'The Unforgettable Fire' (1984) (No.1 in the UK), 'The Joshua Tree' (1987) (No.1 in UK and first No.1 LP in the US) and 'Rattle and Hum' (1988) but while 'The Joshua Tree' often heads polls of "The best U2 album", 'Achtung Baby' is a clear rival for that top spot.

I believe it is their best LP as, given the deliberate change in direction they pursued and, despite the tortuous journey they went on to achieve it, it was still a huge success.

It also revolutionised U2 and freed them from the shackles of the traditional rock sound.

'Rattle and Hum' was a hybrid of live and new songs that truly put U2 on the global map, scoring No.1 chart positions in the UK, US, Australia, Germany, France and Spain; and the third single taken from the LP 'Desire' was their first UK No.1 too.

But its massive commercial success (it shifted 14million copies worldwide) came with criticism towards the album and the film that accompanied it, drawing comments such as 'pretentious' and 'bombastic'.

Drummer Larry Mullen Jnr. admitted they were "the biggest band, but not the best" while Bono told fans at a live show in 1989 it was the "end of something for U2", and they needed to dream it all up again.

The band took a hiatus and wrestled with themselves to climb that creative peak, and ultimately reinvent themselves.

'Achtung Baby' then, was to take a darker, more introspective direction while the group abandoned their rock cliched image for a more light-hearted and self-deprecating one.

The sound of it had probably been born in early 1990 when Bono and the Edge worked on the score for a theatre production of 'A

Clockwork Orange', with music, inspired by industrial bands, that was more avant-garde than U2's traditional sound.

'Alex Descends into Hell for a Bottle of Milk/Korova 1' - eventually the B-side to 'The Fly' - was included in that score.

Indeed, 'Achtung Baby' took on a more European feel, incorporating influences from alternative rock and industrial bands like Nine Inch Nails, to electronic dance music.

Hiring Daniel Lanois and Brian Eno as producers, U2 decamped to Hansa Studios in Berlin where Bowie and Eno had created classic albums in the late 70s/early 80s.

U2 went looking for energy and inspiration following the collapse of the Berlin Wall and German reunification, but instead found a country in a state of dilapidation and a recording studio in need of a makeover, with outdated equipment.

Worse still, the recording sessions for 'Achtung Baby' nearly tore the band apart.

Their time in Berlin was fraught with conflict amid tensions over a shift in musical direction and concerns over the quality of their songs.

For example, Adam Clayton and Larry Mullen Jnr felt pushed out by Bono and the Edge writing songs more closely together and threatened by the use of drum machines as the Edge pursued his new passion for dance music and an industrial sound.

But one song came out of the Berlin sessions that Clayton later reflected on as a "baptism of fire" for the group that salvaged their spirits and brought them back together.

That song was 'One', which went on to be one of U2's most memorable songs.

'One' was borne out of a chord progression that was first linked to an early version of 'Mysterious Ways' which all four improvised on, restoring their faith in their collective output.

Bono cemented the moment in his lyric which is undoubtedly a metaphor for the band: "We're one, but we're not the same. We get to carry each other."

U2 returned to Dublin where it was make or break time.

Fortunately they all decided they did want to carry on with the group and they set about more sessions at Elsinore, a manor in a suburb of their home city.

The tracks 'The Fly', 'Ultraviolet (Light My Way)' and 'Zoo Station', emerged from the recordings. While recording 'The Fly', Bono would sport a pair of over-sized sunglasses, a persona he carried on on the subsequent tour.

'Achtung Baby' got its title from the German word for attention or "watch out" while baby meant the new birth of something.

The phrase "achtung baby" was also coined by a sound engineer during the recording.

After some final work and mixing involving previous U2 producer Steve Lillywhite, U2 were finally happy with their revolutionary record.

'Zoostation' sets the tone for the album, opening it with distorted guitar slides and drums to make listeners think it's a broken CD but by Bono's "ooh aah" you know it's U2.

Lyrically, the track puts the listener aboard a train to an unknown destination.

It sets the scene for a musical journey alighting somewhere rather exciting, and excitingly different.

Bono's distorted vocal declares they are "Ready to let go of the steering wheel" while being "ready for what's next, ready to duck..and dive."

Five songs were released as singles - 'The Fly' which went straight in at No.1 on the UK singles chart in November 1991, 'Mysterious Ways' (1991) that got to No.13, 'One' (March 1992) that hit No.7, 'Even Better Than the Real Thing' (July 1992) that charted at No. 12 (the remix single got to No.8 though) and 'Who's Gonna Ride Your Wild Horses' which was a No.14 hit in December 1992.

But let's face it, the sign of a perfect album is every song could be released as a single and, with songs of the calibre of 'So Cruel' and 'Until The End of the World', 'Achtung Baby' has lifetime membership of that exclusive club.

The LP debuted at No. 1 on the US Billboard albums chart, was No.2 in the UK (kept off top spot by Michael Jackson's 'Dangerous'), went on to sell 18million copies worldwide and win a Grammy, plus it is widely recognised as one of the greatest albums of all time.

Bono by Kirk Whitehouse / Smashed Hits Broken Vinyl.

The Zoo TV tour that followed set the benchmark for future stadium rock shows, pushing the visual and technical limits of the times with a stage set featuring Trabant cars, dozens of large video screens, confessional booths, prank phone calls and guests including everyone from Salman Rushdie to Lou Reed and from Benny and Bjorn from ABBA to Axl Rose.

It also saw Bono recreate his character 'The Fly' as well as those of 'Mr MacPhisto' and 'Mirror Ball Man' as he increasingly self-parodied the rock god persona.

A bold multi-media spectacle, it mimicked the wild antics of morning "zoo" radio and TV shows, was seen by 5.3million people across the world and grossed $151million.

'Achtung Baby' shifted the direction of U2 on to a much more creative and diverse course that helped them maintain relevance and continue to garner acclaim for nearly three more decades, to date.

They had felled 'The Joshua Tree' and planted a forest of new horizons in its place.

• **Check out James' "U is for U2 and My 'Best Of' playlist on Amazon Music at https://amzn.to/3kz6YJX**

"U2 tore down the rock clichés that had formerly enclosed them with 'Achtung Baby', just like the Berlin Wall being pulled down.

"It opened them up to a whole new audience, pushed the boundaries of their musicianship, and the tour that followed re-wrote the rules of live performances."

The sweetest perfection: Why Depeche Mode's 'Violator' remains their finest moment

'V' is for Violator by Depeche Mode

IT was the perfect album, released at the perfect time, and it propelled Depeche Mode to the higher planes of pop music success, putting them on a par with contemporaries like U2 and REM, except 'the Mode' achieved it using synthesizers and samplers.

Celebrating its 30th anniversary this year, 'Violator' was *the* major breakthrough in both the commercial fortunes and critical acclaim of one of my favourite bands, who are frequently misunderstood and criminally underrated.

The seventh studio album by Depeche Mode remains not just my favourite by the legendary synth-rockers, but also my favourite LP of all time.

*

I feel eternally fortunate to have grown up at a time to witness Depeche Mode graduate from the teeny pop of 'See You', through the teenage angst of 'Blasphemous Rumours' and, eventually, into the stadium rock gods they seemed always destined to be with 'I Feel You'.

The epic musical journey of lead singer Dave Gahan, chief songwriter Martin Gore (keyboards, vocals and guitars), Alan Wilder (keyboards, piano and backing vocals) and Andy Fletcher (keyboards and backing vocals), was a joy to witness, and we were lucky to have grown up alongside it.

Having borrowed 'The Singles 81-85' cassette off a girlfriend I was hooked on 'the Mode' and so I taped all Depeche's albums off her, excitedly exploring their impressive back catalogue up to that point, which was circa 1988.

The live album and film '101' - a road movie which builds up to the bands 101st and final show of their 'Music for the Masses' tour in front of 60,000 fans at Pasadena Rose Bowl, filmed by the legendary D.A. Pennebaker - came next.

It was rarely out of the VHS player at my parents' house.
I had become "one of the devout" (that's a line from the Depeche Mode track 'Sacred' for you non-believers!), and so too had my two brothers - it's a bond we still share, decades later.

Depeche Mode were rightly brimming with confidence after the global success of their 'Music of the Masses tour' that preceded the recording of 'Violator'.

While the title of the LP 'Music for the Masses' was intended to be self-deprecating, it had, ironically, been the album that finally brokered large scale international success and set them on the path to 'Violator'.

In between albums, Martin Gore had branched out on a successful solo EP of six cover versions called 'Counterfeit'. Studio whizz Alan Wilder had produced work for Toni Halliday from Curve while industrial favourites Nitzer Ebb were working with soon-to-be Depeche producer Mark 'Flood' Ellis.

Hiring Flood and engineer Francois Kevorkian, Depeche Mode tore up the rule book on their regular working methods, and headed for Milan.

Our copy of Depeche Mode's 'Violator' vinyl, bought the day it came out on 19th March 1990, with sleeve design by Area and photography by Anton Corbijn.

On 'Music for the Masses', Gore had, as per usual, presented the rest of the group with demos of his songs that were almost finished, leaving the band the more simple task of polishing up the songs and adding their own vocals or synth parts.

Ahead of Violator though, Alan Wilder - widely recognised as the 'producer' within Depeche Mode - and co-producer Flood asked

Gore to present his demos in the rawest format possible with just vocals accompanied by either guitar or organ so they could develop the tracks almost from scratch.

The new policy proved a masterstroke.

For example, 'Enjoy The Silence' started life as a slower song with just Martin singing over a simple organ chord sequence. You can hear something very similar on the "Harmonium" version on my playlist.

Andy Fletcher later explained the group had previously lived by restrictive rules in the studio where they would not use the same sound twice and guitars weren't really used. So, for Violator, they stopped all that and declared: "If you wanna use guitars, use guitars."

This afforded them greater creative freedom in the studio with classically-trained Wilder working on sounds and arrangements and Flood offering up the technical expertise on the analogue equipment.

One song that stood out from the early demos was 'Personal Jesus', which saw them break free of their synth-led sound and put down a raunchy blues guitar riff and slide guitars over a glam rock dance stomp.

It was the first time guitars dominated a Depeche Mode track (they had previously appeared fleetingly on tracks like 'Behind The Wheel' (1987) and 'Love In Itself' (1983)), though the deep synth bassline and sampled sounds gave this new track their familiar stamp.

They recorded and released it as their first single off 'Violator' in late August 1989, signposting a bolder and more adventurous sound.

It worked. The 12" single of 'Personal Jesus' - cleverly promoted in newspaper classified ads inviting readers to call a number to reach "Your Own Personal Jesus" which played a segment of the track - became Warner Bros' best selling 12" ever at that point and hyped up anticipation for the new LP.

'Violator' was the first time we'd bought a new Depeche Mode album on vinyl. I clearly remember my brother Matthew coming home from Birmingham city centre on the bus with a copy of it on the day of release - 19th March 1990.

We sat in his bedroom and put the record on. It was a memorable occasion - we couldn't quite believe how brilliant it was.

I felt, even then, we were listening to one of the best recordings we would ever hear.

Little surprise then there was an explosion in popularity of Depeche Mode upon the release of 'Violator'.

The day after the album came out, more than 17,000 screaming fans turned up at a record signing at Wherehouse Records in LA which the private security firm could not handle, and riot police were called in.

There was not a riot, but the ensuing chaos of a massive crowd rushing to see their heroes hit the headlines on US TV from coast to coast in scenes the news anchors likened to Beatlemania.

It was the kind of publicity money could not buy.

Thankfully for the band this was no false dawn, and those whose interest was piqued by what all the fuss was about were duly treated to a perfect Depeche Mode album.

Having heard all of the 12" mixes of 'Personal Jesus' the previous summer and bought 'Enjoy The Silence' the month before, we knew there were at least two tracks of brilliance on 'Violator'.

The superb B-sides to those singles - 'Dangerous' on 'Personal Jesus', and 'Sibeling' and 'Memphisto', the two excellent instrumentals on 'Enjoy The Silence' - shouted out that if they could spare those tracks, there must be some absolute belters on the album.

There were. And the truth is all nine songs on the LP could have been singles.

Indeed, thanks to the Anton Corbijn-directed music video collection 'Strange Too' that accompanied the album, 'Halo' and 'Clean' also got a visual version, in addition to the promo videos for singles 'Enjoy The Silence', 'Personal Jesus', 'World In My Eyes' and 'Policy of Truth'. So, seven songs off 'Violator' were in effect 'released'.

The album also includes the brilliant unlisted linking tracks 'Interlude #2 - Crucified' and 'Interlude #3', that highlight the wealth of wonderful melodies Depeche Mode had on tap at the time.

On the final single to be taken from the album, 'World In My Eyes' we were spoiled again - this time to the sensual dance track 'Sea of Sin' and lusty tones of 'Happiest Girl'.

This truly was a purple patch for Depeche Mode's Ivor Novello-winning chief songwriter Martin Gore.

Let's talk more about the 'Violator' album tracks that make it so perfect.

'World In My Eyes' - The album opener became the fourth single to be released from the LP (No.17 in September 1990).

Andy Fletcher has often called this his favourite of all the Depeche Mode songs, recalling how it came together so well in the studio.

It's Gahan singing but Gore saying, in his eyes, sex and pleasure are positive things to enjoy.

The song has a classic intro with the analogue bass riff before those Kraftwerk-esque snare drum samples and blippy riffs resonate over soothing string samples.

I love the reversed loop before the "And that's all there is" bridge which has a spine-tingling, dramatic chord sequence.

The single video features the only officially-released footage from the 'World Violation Tour'.

'Sweetest Perfection' - 'Real' drums gradually pirouette their way in to the soundscape of this brooding slower song of surrender to an irresistible force, sung by Gore.

Whether it's wine, women or substances (or all three) that he's powerless to resist is open to interpretation.

Whatever it is "Takes me completely, Touches so sweetly, Reaches so deeply, I know that nothing can stop me."

Discordant noises whirl around with guitar slides above the verses as the intoxication takes hold.

A beautiful string segment acts as a release to the desperate intensity of the song.

'Personal Jesus' - Gore told *Rolling Stone* the song was inspired by 'Elvis and Me', Priscilla Presley's memoir. "It's about how Elvis was her man and mentor... everybody's heart is like a god in some way, and that's not a very balanced view of someone, is it?"

It became an instant classic and tens of thousands still "reach out and touch faith", arms aloft, at Depeche shows.

A No.13 hit in the UK in 1989, it's been covered by Marilyn Manson and Johnny Cash (much to the band's delight!)

'Halo' - Gore wrestles with the guilt "like shackles on your feet" of his immoralities on this dramatic and powerful song which sees the unlikely marriage of drums secondhand sampled from Led Zep's John Bonham with strings sampled from Elgar.

It is testament to the great body of work that is 'Violator' that 'Halo' has been played live 431 times by the group since the album came out, despite it not being a single (though it was on their shortlist, and, as previously mentioned, does feature as a video release on 'Strange Too').

'Waiting For The Night' - This beautiful duet of Gahan and Gore's vocal harmonies, set over simple, hypnotic arpeggios from an ARP 2600 synth/ sequencer adds calm to the running order.

Their performance of it on the 2001 'Exciter' tour, remains one of the best Gahan/Gore joint vocal performances I have seen in the many Depeche gigs I've been to.

'Enjoy The Silence' - Gore presented a simple, organ-based song in the demo. Wilder and Flood had different ideas.

They looped a house beat under an analogue bass sequence and programmed in the chords Martin had written.

Next they asked him to work on some guitar licks to overlay on the track.

Memorable results and anthemic melodies ensued, and the rest is history.

Enjoy The Silence was a No.6 hit in the UK in February 1990, becoming gold certified, and it also won Best British Single at the 1991 Brit Awards.

It remains one of their most iconic and popular songs - certainly one of my favourite songs ever - and a key part of their live encore with Martin Gore adding guitar solos in an extended version.

'Policy of Truth' - Another classic Depeche Mode single, peaking at No.15 in the US and No.16 in the UK, the lyrics get straight on topic, questioning whether being truthful is always the best policy.

"Hide what you have to hide, And tell what you have to tell," is the conclusion by the final verse.

The single was backed by the on-trend house track 'Kaleid', a version of which opened the 'World Violation' tour.

Blue Dress' - Gore admits this is "a bit pervy" as it's a simply an open realisation watching his favourite lady put on his favourite blue dress, "the one that he prefers", is "what makes the world turn."

'Clean' - An epic ending to an epic album. The irony of the lyrics "The cleanest I've been" have never been lost on me as this is the point in Depeche Mode history around the time Gahan's near-fatal heroin addiction began.

The bass guitar sample-driven intro is akin to Pink Floyd's 'One of These Days' and the video on the 'Strange Too' collection features Gore watching 'Clean' being painted on a surface on a home movie screen, before spending most of the song kissing a woman.

*

I've debated many times with my Mode mates which is the best album - 'Violator', its raunchier, rockier cousin 'Songs of Faith and Devotion' that followed in 1993, or even 1987's 'Music For The Masses'.

I always (narrowly) side with 'Violator' on this important pop music matter. It's a fine line though.

It's true the title 'Violator' was intended as a joke, as it was the most extreme and ridiculous heavy metal name they could think of.

However, it became a huge international success for Depeche Mode, their first album to chart inside the Billboard 200 in the US, going on to sell 3million copies worldwide.

The 'Violator' era was also the first time my elder brother and I saw them live.

A collage of some of my own Depeche Mode postcards I would have bought from The Oasis in Birmingham in the 1990s.

It was at Birmingham NEC in November 1990, on the final date of their seven-month-long 'World Violation Tour'. (We've seen them at least once on every tour since.)

We were fully invested in Depeche Mode, even dressing in the white 501 jeans, Chelsea boots and biker jackets favoured by frontman Dave Gahan at the time!

Matthew's subscription to "Bong", the Depeche Mode fan club magazine, also meant we got tickets to a huge fan convention at The Institute in Birmingham in 1991. He still has his "Bong Brum" T-shirt!

We also left that night with arms full of cardboard promotional placards for the album which adorned our bedroom walls for many years after.

Exciting times, and 'Violator' was the soundtrack to it all.

Thirty years on and the album still sounds as precise, well crafted and fresh as it did back in 1990. A true testament to its incredible quality.

My top three 'Violator' tracks

1) Enjoy The Silence
2) Personal Jesus
3) World In My Eyes
Underrated track = Sweetest Perfection

• Check out James' "V is for Violator" playlist on Amazon at tinyurl.com/y6b4etqm

Devotee - Me with my very own Depeche Mode Broken Vinyl artwork by my friend Kirk Whitehouse. This one is based on the 'SOFAD' album era though, not 'Violator' !

"Let's be honest, I was always going to write about Depeche Mode somewhere in this book.

"They are my joint favourite group with Pet Shop Boys and have been the soundtrack to my life - lucky me.

"Violator is narrowly my favourite Depeche LP, only just pipping 'Songs of Faith and Devotion', which itself is a masterclass of an album, and, some days, can be top of the list too.

"I just feel 'Violator' is perfect."

The Wonder of Stevie - A child prodigy who became one of the world's greatest ever musicians

'W' is for Wonder

A CHILD prodigy who went blind shortly after birth, Stevie Wonder was born Stevland Hardaway Morris (nee Judkins) on May 13, 1950 in Saginaw, Michigan.

In spite of his disability, Stevland Morris, who later moved to Detroit with his family, became a talented multi-instrumentalist, most noted for his keyboard and harmonica playing, as well as being a top drummer.

Morris was snapped up by Tamla records aged 11, and renamed 'Little Stevie Wonder' by label bosses as he started to rub shoulders with some of the biggest names in R&B like Ray Charles and Smokey Robinson, who Wonder co-wrote 'Tears Of A Clown' for, when he was just 16.

It was not long before Wonder would lose the 'little' tag and grow bigger than his heroes as he matured into one of the greatest singer-songwriters, performers and producers in the history of music.

In the 1970s, Stevie Wonder's critical success was at its peak as he forged a new path for his record label Tamla (Motown) when he pioneered the album format as a mainstay of record sales.

Wonder's LPs 'Innervision (1973), 'Fulfillingness' First Finale' (1974) and 'Songs in the Key of Life' (1976) all won the Grammy for

Album of the Year, making him the tied-record holder for the most wins - with three, and he remains the only artist to have won the title with three consecutive LP releases.

While the 70s saw his critical peak, the 1980s saw Wonder's commercial fortunes flourish and fame explode as he scored chart-topping hit singles around the world, eventually being inducted into the Rock and Roll Hall of Fame in 1989.

Wonder has sold more than 100million albums worldwide and won 25 Grammy awards (including a Lifetime Achievement gong) - the most achieved by any solo artist, and he remains Motown's biggest selling artist ever.

His pioneering use of synthesizers and new technology led to a friendship with American inventor Ray Kurzweil which prompted him to launch his own brand of electronic keyboards in 1982.

Now aged 70, Wonder is a political activist and a United Nations Messenger of Peace. In 2014, he was honoured with the Presidential Medal of Freedom.

*

Stevie Wonder famously sang how he was <u>not</u> superstitious in his 1972 hit song, so here's 13 of my favourite tracks by this musical legend:-

'Uptight (Everything's Alright)' (1966) - After Wonder's No.1 success with 'Fingertips' in 1963, the teenage star was in danger of being let go by Tamla (later Motown) after a string of also-ran releases, so this massive breakthrough hit was a real career-saver.

It was his first co-write - aged just 16 - it hit No.1 in the US (No.14 in the UK) and became a Motown classic that shone the way forward for him as the brilliant songwriter he became.

'Signed, Sealed, Delivered I'm Yours' (1970) - The first song he produced for himself, this co-write, partly credited to his mother Lula Mae Hardway, was a No.1 hit on the US R&B chart and hit No. 15 in the UK (certified Platinum).

It's a timeless hit pop song that crossed over to the mainstream from R&B, and has been covered by other artists more than 100 times. Wonder even scored a No.11 UK chart hit with a new version recorded with Blue and Angie Stone in 2003.

'Superstition' (1972) - Probably the funkiest pop song ever, and arguably his best song, Wonder's exceptional playing on his Hohner Clavinet is only outdone by the fact he puts in another stellar vocal performance. Oh, he also played the Moog bass and the drums on this No.1 US hit (No.11 in the UK)!

The song is saying there's no need to be superstitious, or to have superstitions. Wonder is saying he doesn't believe in them and when you believe in things you don't understand, then you end up suffering anyway.

'Living For The City' (1974) - An absolutely straight to the point social commentary, about the struggles of a young kid who moves from "hard time Mississippi" to New York and ends up in jail, won a Grammy for best R&B song and was taken from the album 'Innervisions' which itself won a Grammy for Album of the Year.

Stevie Wonder has won 25 Grammy awards (including a Lifetime Achievement gong) - the most achieved by any solo artist, and he remains Motown's biggest selling artist ever.

The production and playing on this track is phenomenal, capturing the latest synthesizer sounds, which Wonder was a pioneer of and, once again, it was all played and sung by the maestro himself.

A No.8 Billboard hit in the US (No.15 in the UK), there's a tremendous sense of working class pride despite poverty and prejudice in the moving lyrics: "Her clothes are old but never are they dirty."

'He's Misstra Know-It-All' (1974) - A top ten hit in the UK, this tale of a confidence trickster - "a man with a plan with a counterfeit dollar in his hand" - is alleged to be a reference to President Nixon.

Featuring flute-like sounds from the TONTO synthesizer, it's all Wonder's amazing musicianship again on this great song, with Willie Weeks the only other musician credited, helping out on bass guitar.

'Love's In Need of Love Today' (1976) - Being an 80s child, the first time I heard this classic song was when George Michael dueted on it with Wonder in 1985. Michael later recorded it for the B-side of his No.1 hit single 'Father Figure' in 1988.

Wonder again played nearly all the instruments on his original recording, with the lyrics purveying a message of peace and love needed to be fed more love as "Hate's goin' round, Breaking many hearts." It opens his classic double LP 'Songs In The Key of Life'.

'I Wish' (1976) - Famously sampled by Will Smith for his 1999 hit 'Wild Wild West', this was the first single off 'Songs In The Key of Life' (1977) - widely regarded as the pinnacle of his classic period of recording in the 1970s - that won him a Grammy for best R&B Performance.

'I Wish' was his fifth US No.1 and a No.5 in the UK. The song tells the story of childhood memories and having fun, despite growing up in poverty.

'Isn't She Lovely' (1977) - This adorable ode to the birth of Wonder's daughter Aisha Morris (she's now 45) is another staple hit in his impressive back catalogue.

He refused to cut the 6 minutes 34 seconds long album version (from 'Songs In The Key Of Life') for release as a US single as it contained a recording of his daughter's voice on it he didn't want edited out, and who can blame him.

'Sir Duke' (1977) - This tribute to jazz legend Duke Ellington, that also refers to Count Basie, Glenn Miller, Louis Armstrong and Ella Fitzgerald, was a No.1 hit in the US and No.2 in the UK, and is also taken from 'Songs In The Key Of Life.'

Following Ellington's death in 1974, Wonder wanted to capture in song those musicians he felt were important. He repeated such tributes, to other influential artists, in some of his later hits.

'As' (1977) - The Rhodes piano playing on this track is a masterclass featuring Herbie Hancock combining with Stevie Wonder to create a mellow jazzy groove on top of this brilliant ballad.

There's a few interpretations of the deeper, spiritual meanings of the lyrics but on the surface, they depict one lover saying to another "I'll love you until life and the universe themselves cease to exist."

It's another cracker from the amazing 'Songs In The Key Of Life' LP, which was famously later covered by Stevie Wonder superfan

George Michael and Mary J. Blige, reaching No.4 in the UK in 1999.

'Master Blaster (Jammin')' (1980) - Wonder pays homage to Bob Marley in this reggae pop hit that set him off on a great start to the most commercially successful decade of his career.

The first single off 'Hotter Than July' (1980), it was a big global hit, reaching No.1 in many countries, including Austria, Sweden and New Zealand, topping the US Hot Soul Singles chart and getting to No.2 in the UK, being kept off top spot by The Police's 'Don't Stand So Close To Me'.

'Happy Birthday' (1981) - The third song in my list which pays its respects to one of Stevie Wonder's heroes is this homage to Martin Luther King Jr., which was another UK. No. 2 hit upon its release in April 1981.

A go-to record at birthday parties, the message here was actually more political. Wonder used the song to fight for a holiday on Luther King Jr.'s birthday.

President Reagan eventually approved the creation of the holiday in 1983, and so the official Martin Luther King Jr. Day has been held every January 20 since 1986.

The first commemoration was marked with a big concert, headlined by Wonder.

'I Just Called To Say I Love You' (1984) - Apparently-serious music critics often overlook this saccharin sweet but inch perfect pop song which won an Oscar for Best Original Song (from the 'Woman in Red' soundtrack) on lists like this one.

Fact is it's Wonder's (and Motown's) biggest selling single ever, having topped the charts in no less than 19 countries, including the UK (his only solo No.1 in the UK) and was his eighth No.1 in the US.

'I Just Called...' sees Wonder perform all the parts once again, and embracing new synthesizer technology, like the vocoder effect he achieved with a Roland VP-330, and a Linn drum machine.

It's one of the best pop songs ever recorded, and I mean it from the bottom of my heart.

• Check out James' 'W is for Stevie Wonder' playlist on Amazon Music at https://amzn.to/324W1Za

"Fond memories of listening to Stevie Wonder on my old pal Al's record decks, round at his parents' house when we were kids.

"His dad had all the LPs on vinyl and generously let us listen to them.

"That was my first big slice of Motown. I also loved Wonder's 1980s recordings which made excellenet use of synthesizer and sequencer technology, showing again what a pioneer he is."

How 'X&Y' cracked the code for Coldplay's global success

'X&Y' is for Coldplay's 'X&Y' album

ONE of the brightest new bands of the new millennium, Coldplay burst on to the music scene in 2000 with their monster hit 'Yellow', while their No.1 debut album 'Parachutes' was nominated for the Mercury Prize.

Formed at University College London in 1996, Chris Martin (vocals and piano), guitarist Jonny Buckland, bass player Guy Berryman and drummer Will Champion, have sold more than 100million records worldwide, won nine Brits, seven Grammys and countless MTV awards.

Now an established stadium tour and Glastonbury-headlining act, it was Coldplay's 'X&Y' album, which marked its 15th anniversary this year, that put the four-piece on the pathway to becoming one of the biggest bands in the world.

*

'PARACHUTES' had been an impressive landing in the indie-pop sphere for Coldplay, having peaked at No.1, and featuring great singles like 'Shiver', 'Yellow', 'Trouble' and 'Don't Panic'.

The debut LP sold 8.5million copies, went nine times platinum and won the Brit Award for Best British Album in 2001.

Follow-up album 'A Rush of Blood To The Head' (2002), featuring the brilliant singles 'In My Place' (a No.2 hit), 'The Scientist', 'Clocks' and 'God Put A Smile Upon Your Face', went straight to the top of the UK album charts, spawned three Grammys, won Best British Album again at the 2003 Brit Awards, and also went nine times platinum on these shores.

It was a No.1 album around the world and remains their best-selling studio LP.

Coldplay were on the crest of a wave critically and commercially, they had headlined the Pyramid stage at Glastonbury in 2002, but suddenly found themselves needing to regroup and plan that "difficult third album".

After their initial pop successes, the band spent most of 2004 out of the spotlight, taking a break from touring and promotion while trying to record the perfect record.

The sessions that followed, and there were plenty of them, eventually became 'X&Y' - a title Chris Martin later explained to mean a kind of "ying and yang - a mixture of optimism and pessimism."

The recording of 'X&Y' was not without its difficulties, but that's exactly why it pushed Coldplay on to the next level in terms of their credibility and global appeal.

They intended to make "the best record anyone had ever heard" and were determined to get it right, no matter what it took.

That's partly why, after initially working again with Ken Nelson - the producer of their first two albums, they scrapped 52 of the 60 songs they had written, citing their dissatisfaction with them.

They had been rehearsing songs for upcoming live shows and felt their live versions sounded better than what they had recorded. Guitarist Jonny Buckland said they felt they sounded like they were going backwards, compared to their first two albums.

Determined to fix the problem, the group eventually worked with Danton Supple, who had been an engineer on 'A Rush Of Blood..', and the version we now know as 'X&Y' is in fact the third version of the album they produced.

The release date was pushed back from 2004 to 2005 to accommodate their desire for perfection and even Brian Eno was brought in to play synthesizer on the song 'Low' - a telling moment as Eno went on to produce their next LP 'Viva La Vida...' (2008).

Indeed, his influence, and that of other electronic artists like Kraftwerk (on 'Talk'), can be heard on 'X&Y' as more synthesizers and samples were added to the atmosphere.

Drummer Will Champion said they had not been under pressure, wanting to create the best record they could, but setting themselves a deadline of early 2005 to finish the LP did focus their efforts on finalising the tracks for 'X&Y', which I will now discuss in more detail.

The group eventually settled on **'Square One'** to open the album, a song which Martin hailed as a call to arms for he and his

Coldplay are now one of the biggest bands in the world, renowned for their epic live shows and have sold more than 100 million records globally. Picture by Frank Schwichtenberg, used under Creative Commons Licence.

band-mates, with its apt lyrics wanting to decipher the codes (to life itself, or their next musical move?).

Martin issues an emotive plea for the journey ahead: "I need a compass, draw me a map, I'm on the top, I can't get back."

'What If' - This philosophical and fragile piano-led ballad starts out rather pessimistically pondering whether he is about to get things wrong or right, highlighting self-doubt, but it builds to a warmer, more confident feel as strings are mixed up into the track.

'White Shadows' - This was to be the final single released off 'X&Y', though only as a radio single in Mexico to coincide with their Latin America tour of 2007.

The haunting organ chords are significant, hovering above a typical Coldplay guitar and drum-led song, but adding a new layer to their latest sound.

Lyrically, it reflects on younger days and philosophizes our place in the universe.

Are we part of a system or a bigger plan we can't comprehend? Either way, the song is optimistic enough to hope that the 'White Shadows' always "sparkle and glisten".

'Fix You' - A stone-cold Coldplay classic, 'Fix You' begins as a calming organ ballad but develops into an indie-rock upbeat tempo chorus for the "Tears streaming down on your face, When you lose something you can't replace" part before Martin promises the troubled soul(s): "I will try to fix you."

A No.4 hit in September 2005, 'Fix You' is a highly emotional and beautiful song, and it's one of my favourites of theirs. I love the way it deals with a tragic situation but ultimately offers hope and help to the suffering party.

Martin later said it was probably the most important song they had ever written.

'Talk' - The band got permission from Kraftwerk to use the riff from their 1981 hit 'Computer Love' which works so well with this rapid track.

The third single from 'X&Y', it peaked at No.10 in the UK singles chart and is another song where the narrator offers guidance in an uncertain time to anyone who "feels like a puzzle" or "can't find their missing piece."

'X&Y' - The axis point of the LP, it sits at the close of the 'X' side of the album and again, the lyrics revisit the promise to fix or repair a broken situation anyway they can. There's a sense of helplessness in the notion they are "drifting on a tidal wave" or "floating into outer space."

'Speed Of Sound' - A No.2 UK hit when it was released as the first single off the LP in April 2005, 'Speed Of Sound' is a sibling to 'Clocks' given its piano arpeggio-driven motifs and perhaps the song off 'X&Y' that's closest sounding to their previous album.

The synthesizer-heavy orchestral chords add an ethereal feel to the song while the rumbling drums are reminiscent of Kate Bush's hit 'Running Up That Hill.'

Kicking off the 'Y' side of 'X&Y', it won a Brit Award for Best British Single in 2006.

'A Message' - The haunting synth pads are back with a message "you don't have to be on your own", which was inspired by Martin's favourite hymn 'My Song Is Love Unknown', written by English composer John Ireland in 1664.

Martin admits there's a definite church influence on the band given all the school assemblies they sat through, and he wrote this one out of nowhere (like several of the songs on the album) after waking up in the middle of the night!

'Low' - A definite U2 vibe emerges on this Eno-influenced track (the legendary producer played backing synths on it too) which comments on the ups and downs of a relationship attempting to live in perfect symmetry, reiterating that "ying and yang" theme that permeates the album.

'The Hardest Part' - Joyful piano playing dominates this great song, written by all four band members, which pays tribute to REM and was a radio-only single in the UK.

Feeling and sounding a bit like REM's 'Losing My Religion', 'The Hardest Part' is a triumphant slice of accessible pop-rock.

'Swallowed In The Sea' - Anthemic yet sincere, I feel this should have been a single as it is a very sweet love song saying: "You belong with me, not swallowed in the sea."

I love the unconditional hope of the lines: "The streets you're walking on, A thousand houses long, Well, that's where I belong, And you belong with me."

'Twisted Logic' - The track that lent its name to the series of live shows that followed the 'X&Y' album has rarely been performed live, not even on that tour, which is in itself a "twisted logic."

It features deep Rickenbacker guitar arpeggios akin to those on The Beatles' 'I Want You (She's So Heavy)', which, of course, is no bad thing.

'Till Kingdom Come' - The album's 'hidden track' as it was originally just listed as the '+' symbol on the inside track listings (and not at all on the sleeve), this was originally planned as a duet with Johnny Cash, but the country legend died before the recording could be made.

It did, however, get pride of place in the hit superhero movie 'The Amazing Spider-Man', several years later in 2012, and is another beautiful love song full of hope and blind optimism. "For you, I've waited a thousand years," Martin declares.

'X&Y' set Coldplay apart from contemporaries and, in succeeding in making a perfect record, they shifted to a trajectory of wider world success, paving the way for all the great albums that have followed.

Strong and accomplished, it debuted at No.1 in 20 countries and was the best-selling album of 2005 (shifting more than 13million copies to date), while it firmly established them of the band of the decade.

'X&Y' scooped the Best British Album award at the 2006 Brits and was their third successive Mercury Prize nomination.

Five chart-topping albums have followed, each taking on a bold individual feel while retaining that Coldplay sound, and each time further cementing their enduring global appeal.

The future's for discovering.

My top three songs on 'X&Y'

1. Fix You
2. Swallowed In The Sea
3. The Hardest Part
Underrated track = Til Kingdom Come

• Check out James' 'X&Y is for Coldplay and My Best Of' playlist on Amazon Music at https://amzn.to/2RvREBB

"Coldplay can be a 'Marmite' band, but you can't deny their high status in the pop world. They didn't fluke their way to the top.

"Their success stems from good songwriting, talented musicianship, and their desire to be at the absolute peak of everything they do.

"Coldplay's live shows are phenomenal too."

John Bonham's incredible legacy lives on, 40 years after his death

'Z' is for Led Zeppelin

"THE MOST outstanding and original drummer of his time, John Bonham's popularity and influence continue to resonate within the world of music and beyond."

Those are the poignant words that grace a 2.5tonne bronze statue in Mercian Square, Redditch, the home town of John Bonham, who was born on May 31, 1948 and began playing drums at the tender age of five.

Bonham tragically died 40 years ago - on September 25, 1980 - aged just 32, but his reputation as a drummer has grown beyond hard rock following his death, and he is now seen as one of the greatest drummers of all time.

*

Born on Birchfield Road in Redditch, Worcestershire, John Henry Bonham (named after his father and grandfather) began learning to play drums at five, making a kit out of containers and coffee tins.

His younger sister Deborah recalled in a radio interview how, even before young John could walk, he just wanted to hit pots and pans, often driving his mother Joan mad!

Despite that, Bonham received a snare drum off his mum when he was ten, followed by a full kit off his dad when he was 15, upon which he would imitate his idols, including Max Roach, Gene Krupa, and Buddy Rich.

He never took formal drum lessons, picking up tips from fellow drummers instead. He became well known on the local gig circuit as a talented stickman, taking his pick of the up-and-coming bands to play with.

In 1964, Bonham became semi-professional with Terry Webb and the Spiders, and met his future wife Pat Phillips around this time. He then took up drumming full time with other Brummie bands like The Senators, playing on their single 'She's A Mod' (1964).

A couple of years later, he joined A Way Of Life but after their demise he hooked up with a blues band called Crawling King Snakes, whose leader singer was a curly haired chap called Robert Plant.

Plant remembered the first time they met, saying Bonham had an "arrogant air" about him and was quite cocky!

"John told me: 'You're pretty good, but you'd be better if you had a drummer like me!" Plant recalled in a radio interview.

Despite the prickly initial assessment, Plant and Bonham went on to forge a dynamic relationship in Led Zeppelin and had a mutual respect for each other.

Before that there were a few switch arounds with the bands they each performed in, including Bonham playing for Tim Rose's group, before Jimmy Page left The Yardbirds.

Plant and Page formed another band (initially called The New Yardbirds) and they set about hiring Bonham, but he was not keen at first.

Page and manager Peter Grant had seen Bonham play for Tim Rose and soon saw what Plant had already recognised in the formidable drummer.

Dozens of telegrams were sent to Bonham's local pub in Bloxwich - at the same time he was getting more lucrative offers from the likes of Joe Cocker and Chris Farlowe - but he eventually decided he liked Page and Plant's music better so they got their man.

Joining the three in the band that became Led Zeppelin was another big talent, the bass and keyboard player John Paul Jones.

Led Zeppelin drew their influences from rock, blues and folk but were among the forefathers of heavy metal, along with the likes of Deep Purple, Black Sabbath, Rush, Queen, Aerosmith and Megadeth who followed.

Even in more recent years, alternative rock bands like the Smashing Pumpkins, Nirvana, Pearl Jam and Soundgarden have cited the Zep as a major influence.

Led Zeppelin went on to sell more than 200million records and released eight studio albums from 'Led Zeppelin' and 'Led Zeppelin II' (both 1969) through to 'In Through The Out Door' (1979), heralding the era of the album and stadium tour bands in the process.

Their untitled fourth studio album - famous for the quartet's "symbols" on the sleeve and commonly known as Led Zeppelin IV (1971) - became one of the best-selling albums in history.

The LP contained 'Stairway to Heaven', which is one the most popular and influential songs in rock music as well as the superb 'Rock and Roll' and 'When The Levee Breaks'.

"Bonzo", as he was affectionately known, was renowned for his fast, loud and heavy drum sound, together with his incredible kick drum play.

He was the powerhouse that underpinned the heavy metal sound but his playing was much more intricate than that, and that's why he's still seen as the world's best ever drummer.

He had been initially influenced by listening to the likes of Joe Morello from the Dave Brubeck Quartet, Buddy Rich and Gene Krupa on his parents' jazz records as a kid.

Such early inspirations shone through in Bonham's drumming technique.

There was no second kick drum being used. He would replace the strap for a chain on his Ludwig kit's bass drum, and many contemporaries soon followed, having been left dumbfounded by his impressive triplet fills which were akin to those great jazz players.

Star stickman - Bonzo at work behind his drum kit. Picture via Wikipedia, used under Creative Commons Licence.

Bonzo threw in accents and could create a groove like funk drummers such as Clyde Stubblefield who worked with James Brown.

It's often been said that Led Zeppelin didn't just have a lead singer and a lead guitarist, but also a lead bassist and a lead drummer. That's what set them apart.

Indeed, on tracks like 'Immigrant Song' (1970), you can hear how Bonham's drums are like a lead track as they echo Page's lead guitar riffs, rather than working exclusively with John Paul Jones' bassline.

On 'Fool In The Rain' (1979) the separate hi-hat track and snare / kick track work together as two complementary rhythms before a calypso middle section begins.

'Kashmir' (1975) pits Bonham's 4/4 time rock beat against the strings and guitar working more in triplets, so they only sync up every 12 beats, which builds a dramatic tension.

Perhaps the best showcase of his drumming is on the brilliant Moby Dick (1969), where a 12-bar blues riff in D intro drops away to let his kit make the melodies for six minutes, though this sometimes became half an hour on live shows!

Marvel at John Bonham playing 'Moby Dick' live in concert on this YouTube clip - https://bit.ly/3hKt5vn

Contemporaries like Black Sabbath drummer Bill Ward said Bonzo set up his drums according to whether or not it felt like you had been punched in the stomach or not. If it felt like you had, he was getting there!

Jimi Hendrix, upon watching Led Zeppelin live in the 70s, said: "That drummer of yours has got a right foot like a pair of castanets!"

Sir Paul McCartney, who worked with Bonzo in Wings, called him a "powerhouse" drummer who was "downright ballsy". They worked together on Wings' 'Beware My Love' track.

Phil Collins said John Bonham "is probably the most important influence in my life", and often tried to emulate his hero on his own recordings.

Dave Grohl says Bonzo will forever be the greatest drummer of all time.

Bandmate John Paul Jones called him a "bass player's dream" while Jimmy Page said Bonham made life easy for producers as he knew how to tune his drums and get so much volume out of them just by playing with his wrists. "He really knew how to make the instrument sing," said Page.

Robert Plant has regularly stated Bonham was irreplaceable and Led Zeppelin could never play again without him. He said Bonzo was the main part of the band, who made it all work.

Writing at the time of Bonham's 70th birthday in 2018, when a bronze sculpture created by Mark Richards was unveiled in his home town of Redditch, fellow journalist Matthew Salisbury wrote about "*John Bonham's fabulous band.*"

Salisbury, who witnessed the mighty Zep performing in the 1970s, described Bonham as a "peerless" player who was: "Powerful, driving, frequently over-the-top and as much a star as the rest of the quartet. He also provided subtlety behind some of the decade's great gentle songs. A true all-rounder.

"While his early death has given him that legend status which always guarantees a place at rock's top table, it should be noted that he won his enviable reputation while very much still alive.

The most outstanding and original drummer of his time - This bronze sculpture created by Mark Richards was unveiled in John Bonham's home town of Redditch on May 31, 2018, which would have been his 70th birthday. Picture by James Iles.

"Perhaps the greatest testament to Bonzo's worth is there in the fact that when he died, so did the band.

"They could have just slid in a replacement and continued to pull in the fans, the sales and the plaudits. But they didn't. And that's something Redditch should be proud of."

*

Led Zeppelin's world and the lives of family, friends and fans came crashing down though when, on September 25, 1980, John Bonham tragically died in his sleep following a day spent drinking vodka during band rehearsals.

A verdict of accidental death was recorded by the coroner and Bonham was laid to rest at Rushock Parish Church, Worcestershire.

Rather than replace Bonham, Led Zeppelin chose to disband out of respect for the "King of the Sticks".

A press release signed "Led Zeppelin", and dated December 4, 1980, stated: "We wish it to be known that the loss of our dear friend and the deep respect we have for his family, together with the sense of undivided harmony felt by ourselves and our manager, have led us to decide that we could not continue as we were."

Still setting the benchmark for rock drummers and topping all the polls (he was ranked in first place by *Rolling Stone* in its list of the "100 Greatest Drummers of All Time"), Bonham was posthumously inducted into the Rock and Roll Hall of Fame in 1995 as a member of Led Zeppelin.

• **Check out James' 'Z is for Led Zeppelin' playlist on Amazon Music at https://amzn.to/2ZJGHk7**

Author's notes on Led Zeppelin:

"I've never seriously classed myself a hard rock or heavy metal fan, and therefore I am guilty of overlooking bands like Led Zeppelin (though of course, they are every bit a folk, blues or even alternative rock band too).

"Writing about John Bonham, and further researching the Zep's music has gone some way to remedying past oversights.

"That's the great thing about pop music - you can go down a rabbit hole with one band or artist and before you know it you've broadened your horizons and discovered even more great songs.

"I really got into them and feel proud to live in the same town (just a few miles away from) where he was born and grew up.

"It's an incredible honour for Redditch to be the birthplace of a true music legend and I feel it is a fitting way to finish my A to Z journey of Hit Artists."

Acknowledgements

This book could not have been illustrated without the help of my long-time friend, the very talented artist Kirk Whitehouse, who generously gave me permission to reproduce photographs of his original Smashed Hits Broken Vinyl artworks. He is available for commission - you'll find him on social media.

All other pictures are credited in the captions next to them and are gratefully acknowledged by the author and publisher.

Every attempt will be made to correct or acknowledge any image that has not been appropriately credited in any future editions of this title.

Special thanks go to my partner Becky for giving me the courage of my convictions to write this book and for my friends Matthew, Neil and Christopher for their support and encouragement too.

Thanks also to my children, Harry, Luke and Beatrice, and my brothers Matthew and Andrew and their families, for their love and support as always. I'm a lucky man.

Finally, thanks to my mom and dad for first introducing me to pop music which has helped to give me such a happy and fulfilled life.

And an extra thanks to 'D' for proof-reading the book for me.

I love you all.